The Wellness Formula

Formula

12 Factors for Cultivating Positively Energized, High Performance Workplaces and Lifestyles

Sarah Deane

ISBN: 978-0-578-40677-0

DEDICATION

To my amazing family, husband, business partner and friends, for always supporting me and inspiring me to be the best version of myself.

"Every living organism is fulfilled when it follows the right path for its own nature."

Marcus Aurelius

CONTENTS

"Life grows relatively to one's investment in it."

Marc Benioff, CEO Salesforce

PREFACE

After numerous years working in the fields of A.I., cognitive and behavioral science and experience design, I found myself embarking on a new chapter in my journey. I knew from the moment I began this path, that I wanted to use my expertise to help people and organizations be their best selves by focusing on the mindsets, behaviors, and environmental factors that enable them to achieve their version of success.

My name is Sarah Deane, and along with James Mulkerin, I created a diagnostic and mindset and behavioral development system which became MEvolution. We created it as we saw a rising gap in how people were able to engage new and healthy behaviors, how they were able to work on mental strength and wellbeing, and an increasing need for resiliency and stress management. When we started all those years ago, there was, and still is, a wealth of information, mobile apps and services around wellbeing, positive psychology, and mindfulness. However, even with all the corporate and individual spend on wellness, fitness, health, and personal development, we were seeing worrying levels of stress, depression, burnout and anxiety. Back in 2017, we came to the quick realization that we could take our proprietary process, of creating accurate and actionable measurement systems used to fast track sustained positive change, and apply it to providing an accessible, approachable solution to this sought-after space. We already had successful systems in the domains of customer experience, employee engagement, leadership, and high-performance cultures, so we thought--could we help people better understand what was holding them back? Could we rapidly and accurately pinpoint what was causing them to feel, well, "bleh" for lack of a better word?

Fast forward a few years, and the answer is yes. We have successfully been able to help people at Fortune 500's and growing start-ups feel more positive, achieve higher levels of performance, and experience sustained behavior change. All with the goal of being able to be healthier, happier, and progress towards their desired future.

This overview aims to take you on a journey through the 12 factors that we found create the mental muscles and behavioral health for resilience, stress management and emotional awareness, as well as the navigation of positive and negative states of being. It is the result of extensive research and our proprietary data modeling process to discover the critical behaviors and indicators based on the successful norms of others.

This book is meant for the individual who wants to understand what may be hindering them from achieving their goals or what may be blocking them from feeling or performing their best. It is for the manager, who wants to understand how they can best support and empower their teams. It is for the leader, who wants to understand how to foster positively energized cultures and how they can elevate their existing wellness and development initiatives with a focus on the core competencies that enable people to feel higher levels of engagement and productivity.

It is also for people that are in high-stress, emotional roller-coaster types of roles, such as founders, high profile individuals, and leadership. Founders experience an emotional journey with many intense ups and downs happening on a daily basis. Providing them with the behaviors that will help them remain focused, feel calm and manage their stress, can help ensure that they can give energy to all of their responsibilities in the best way for themselves, their company, and their loved ones. Leadership plays a vital role in inspiring their employees, demonstrating their company values, and in fostering an engaged and high performing culture. Illuminating their behavioral blockers and their impact, and aligning their individual values so that they can naturally role model the company values, helps to ensure that they drive a positive company culture. Fast-paced teams in high-stress environments (such as customer support, account management or sales) need to stay on their A-game. Regardless of what is happening, they need to remain focused. Understanding how to navigate mental states, cope with challenging moments and increase resilience, keeps these individuals and teams at peak performance.

On a personal level, as we always do with our creations, I have gone through our evaluation process and development system to work on my own opportunities for growth. Having seen the results firsthand, I believe with dedicated focus we can truly improve the wellbeing of our workforces. Given recent years, with stress, depression, and burnout on the rise, strategies and mindsets that promote energizing behaviors are needed now more than ever.

When I received my analysis, I found that one of my areas to work on was paying better attention to my boundaries and ensuring that I cultivated the relationships that mattered. I also found that I had to work on bringing in more basic self-care activities into my daily life. While some of this was hard to hear, especially behaviors regarding fostering relationships, once I started the growth exercises, even I was shocked at the clarity it brought me. Fast forward to now, and I can honestly say that I stop and take in moments of awe, I make a conscious effort to be present, and I handle the challenges of home life and business with a much more purposeful response system. My journey certainly didn't stop there. It takes daily reflection and action to improve and see impact--and I am still using my results today to continue growing.

This book aims to bring you a rapid awareness of the behaviors and mindsets that foster highly energized, productive, and engaged people, so that you can apply it to your own growth, your employee wellbeing initiatives or your leadership development.

I hope the insights are useful in your journey regardless of your level or role!

"New and exciting innovations and technologies have come along to shape our approach to employee wellbeing, but our attitude has always remained the same – it's our people who drive our success, so we strive to maintain a healthy and happy culture, and create environments in which everyone can flourish."

Sir Richard Branson

Introduction

Why is this important?

With burnout, stress, and depression on the rise, it is clear that we are feeling more overwhelmed than ever before. In fact, a national survey of 614 Human Resources (HR) leaders, including CHRO's, VP's, Directors and Managers, found that 95 percent of participants admit that employee burnout is sabotaging workforce retention. It is no wonder that Gallup found that more than half of the U.S workforce is not engaged, the impact of which is not only on individual wellbeing but including massive losses in productivity, costing between $450 and $500 billion a year according to Mental Health America. According to the Harvard Business Review, "in our research over the past decade, we have found that emotional culture influences employee satisfaction, burnout, teamwork, and even hard measures such as financial performance and absenteeism. Countless empirical studies show the significant impact of emotions on how people perform on tasks, how engaged and creative they are, how committed they are to their organizations, and how they make decisions. Positive emotions are consistently associated with better performance, quality, and customer service--this holds true across roles and industries and at various organizational levels. On the flip side (with certain short-term exceptions), negative emotions such as group anger, sadness, fear, and the like usually lead to negative outcomes, including poor performance and high turnover."

In response, we are seeing more and more spent by individuals and organizations, with corporate wellness programs at nearly an 8-billion-dollar industry in the U.S. alone (and forecasted to grow), and 11 billion spent on self-help by Americans alone. There are an ever-increasing amount of applications for health and wellbeing from trackers to content. There are hundreds of thousands of health-related apps, yet, nearly 50 percent of the workforce suffers from burnout and 8/10 Americans are inflicted by stress.

Even though this picture looks so very gloomy, there is a light at the end of the tunnel. In her book "The How of Happiness," psychology professor Dr. Sonja Lyubomirsky lets us know that as much as 40 percent of our happiness can be driven by the intentional activities that we choose to engage in. These activities include things like being absorbed in moments, experiencing joy, acts of kindness, and not dwelling on problems.

One way to help people cope and break through their limiting barriers is to equip them with strategies and tools they can implement to engage new behaviors that leave them feeling more energized, more engaged, and being more productive. By becoming aware of their de-energizing behaviors and mindsets and shifting them to more positive norms, organizations can create healthier individuals and teams.

There are several benefits to both the individual and the organization when people are able to better navigate their positive and negative states and shift into more energizing behaviors. By improving how people manage their energy states, they can experience:

> ***Increased resilience:*** being able to adapt quickly to shifts in the environment, to move past minor setbacks, and being able to stay focused on the bigger goal at hand, enables faster movement into a more productive and positive state.

Sustained happiness: having a grateful mindset enables increased and lasting feelings of fulfillment.

Improved attention and memory: being able to shift how and when energy is spent on different types of tasks can increase the quality of work and output.

Higher levels of ideation: being in less stressed, more positive, and renewed states of mind, enables creative thoughts to flow more easily.

Healthier relationships: being able to understand how personal energy impacts others, and how others can positively or negatively impact energy levels, enables relationships that are meaningful and rewarding to be cultivated.

Reduced levels of inaccurate thoughts: being able to understand what the truthful and accurate reality is, and practicing self-compassion, evokes more positive emotions and a more aligned self-perception.

It is important to realize that our energy fluctuates. In different moments we may experience a myriad of emotions, some may be positive and some negative, each with their own level of intensity. By managing how we respond and understanding how to navigate our mental states, we can train ourselves to stay in a more positive and engaged place.

Our brain's tendency to look for negatives was once vital for human sustainment, and still plays an important role. However, with the overstimulated environment we now live in, we need to manage the constant activation of our fight or flight mode, which stresses our nervous system, causing impact to our attention, focus, memory, and wellbeing. Unfortunately, this can also lead us to overreact to non-threatening moments. The key is in understanding when a situation is non-threatening and how to take a step back and process the situation for the best response.

While learning these skills can have a huge impact on one's personal life, it has been demonstrated that the benefits for an organization are plenty.

Being able to optimize the energizing behaviors of your employees, as well as unlock and manage human capacity, has been seen to positively influence:

- Overall health and wellbeing
- Engagement in work and life
- Productivity and performance
- Workplace culture
- Focus and attention

In fact, studies by Gallup, and other experts, have shown several points of evidence for focusing on employee wellbeing as it pertains to managing positive states such as:

- 41 percent less absenteeism when employees are engaged at work
- 31 percent increase in productivity when a brain is in a positive state versus negative or neutral state
- $3,900 saved per employee that is converted from unhappy to happy (based on average $65,000 salary)
- Companies with happier and engaged employees tend to outperform their competition by 202 percent

But where does an organization even start? It has often been seen that while organizations spend hundreds of millions on measuring things like engagement and program success, there is rarely sustained improvement. As the Harvard Business Review comments, "most initiatives amount to an adrenaline shot. A perk is introduced to boost scores, but over time the effect wears off and scores go back down". There is a lack of understanding across what is needed for sustained impact--what is needed in the environment, what behaviors are needed, and what mindsets are needed--and then programs that follow to cultivate these. While we so often measure to trend, categorize, and compare, organizations rarely have the capability to look at what components impact their desired end state, which in this case is happy, healthy, and productive employees.

The problem is that what companies are doing is not enough to address the underlying issues nor move the needle on engagement, burnout, and stress. Companies are missing a crucial component--the active development of the right behaviors. According to Deloitte, "50 percent of all companies admit their employee development programs are outdated". Most training and development initiatives do not even cover this area or are siloed attempts to cultivate skills. They also tend to lack bringing the practice of the behaviors into the context of an employee's life--professionally or personally. Without practice in context, it is harder to engage new behaviors that become lasting habits. Competencies such as resilience are often missing from employees ongoing growth and development plans. While resilience is not a new concept, it is finding new life and resonance in today's fast-paced, ever-changing, always-on world. In fact, The Harvard Business Review calls resilience the new leadership. Simply, it is the 21st century's organizational survive and thrive capability.

Resilience is the key skill needed for organizations to thrive.

Moreover, it is not just an employee development gap but is something that needs to be planned for at all levels of an organization. Research has demonstrated that a manager's capacity to be resilient is closely related to them having a transformational (rather than transactional) leadership style and positive wellbeing. According to Dr. Jane Gunn, Partner, People & Change, KPMG, "resilience is a central component of one's capacity to lead. It's the ability of leaders to manage their own personal responses and reactions in a fast-paced environment." A problem that has naturally arisen from the complex and competitive environment that all levels of employees, and especially leaders, find themselves in--is the need to multitask. According to Andrew May, Partner at KPMG Performance Clinic, "the technology demands add to cognitive overload, which can impact their memory and processing capacity by 15 percent," a large performance hit for any organization.

However, it is possible to change the way people think. It has been shown that "with thinking skills, 50 percent is genetic, 40 percent is trainable, and 10 percent is lifestyle. You can work on your thinking skills to become more flexible." Cultivating the behaviors and mental muscles, and having leadership that role-model these behaviors, such as the ability to step back, see things from other perspectives, work through challenging situations, and seize opportunities has a huge positive impact on workplace culture.

In addition, people's energy is contagious, so de-energizing behaviors can quickly lead to demotivated employees who are going through the motions, as well as workplace toxicity. In fact, a study by the University of Manchester's Business School recently shows that employees working for a toxic boss experienced lower rates of job satisfaction. Reporting in the Journal of Applied Psychology, Russell Johnson and colleagues found that experiencing such rude behavior reduces employees' self-control and leads them to act in a similar uncivil manner. In fact, their study demonstrated that "people who are recipients of incivility at work feel mentally fatigued as a result, because uncivil behaviors are somewhat ambiguous and require employees to figure out whether there was any abusive intent. This mental fatigue, in turn, led them to act uncivil toward other workers. In other words, they paid the incivility forward."
All of these issues can stem from a lack of focus on growing the underlying behaviors and mental strengths that create a positively energized workforce--where people feel and perform their best.

We have proven that using our novel, proprietary methodology to quickly build a clear and accurate picture of a person's mindset and behavioral blockers, combined with personalized, guided programming and monitoring that fits their life, we can provide expedited and sustained positive impact, leading to more fulfilled, productive, and resilient individuals, teams, and organizations.

Through our research-based modeling process we have discovered the attributes that impact human capacity, that keep people, teams, and organizations at their peak energy levels for optimal performance, emotional wellbeing, and achievement of potential.

What contributes to people feeling positively energized?

We set out to answer the question, "what is needed to perform and feel your best throughout your day?" As a result of our research and data modeling process, we found 74 behavioral and cognitive competencies, which run across 12 factors that contribute to positively energized people.

Accountability: Holding oneself accountable for one's actions, mindset, behaviors, and attitude.

Achievement: Embracing opportunities for growth and learning, setting challenging goals and acknowledging meaningful achievements.

Alignment of Task and Time: Correlating time, energy and efforts to one's purpose, skills, and to what is meaningful.

Authenticity: Acting with compassion, being genuine, and living one's values.

Awareness: Being aware of oneself, others, and one's environment.

Basic Wellbeing and Self Care: Ensuring that basic needs around health and wellbeing are taken care of as well as practicing kindness to oneself and others.

Mindful Practice: Paying attention, being in the present moment, and being non-judgmental.

Positive Outlook: Expressing genuine gratitude and seeing the good in situations and people.

Purpose and Meaning: Being connected to a greater purpose and having a focus on what brings oneself satisfaction.

Relationships: Fostering high quality and authentic connections with others.

Solution Focus: Having the ability to move past frustrating situations and challenging circumstances with a view to growth, learning, and problem-solving.

Support Network: Utilizing a strong support network.

A Word on Behavior Change...

With a topic as complex as this, achieving desired outcomes and sustained impact will take effort and patience. There are lots of behaviors that contribute to being the best version of yourself. However, awareness is the first step in working to close the gap and engage new, energizing behaviors. The good news is, it is never too late to develop the skills, mindsets and behaviors needed to feel and perform your best!

There are a few key components that play a significant role in any program aimed at enabling behavioral change and developing new thought patterns. Being aware of, and utilizing, these core elements can increase the success of any development journey.

1: Focus

Once you understand your openings for growth, it is important to decide the committed actions that you as an individual, as a team, or as an organization, will take. It is imperative to focus on one area or one behavior change at a time and to keep working on it until it is consistent. Trying to change too much at once can lead to less progress, which has a negative emotional effect that can deter one's path. For example, when trying to lose weight, someone with the best of intentions could try and start working out 5 days a week, eating no carbs, and give up drinking alcohol. Then, with all the change and long work hours they start slipping up, which leads to a binge eating day. This leads to feelings of "what's the point?!" which causes them to give up.

Or, perhaps a leader who wants to better connect with their employees commits to weekly one-on-ones with their team members, in which they are not distracted by their emails. However, when reality hits they find the task to be too challenging given their responsibilities. This may make them end up feeling worse about themselves, as well as making the team members feel badly also. In this case, it may have been better to have taken a small step, maybe once a month, or something that is more realistic and achievable.

When looking to engage new behaviors, just take it in small steps at a time, and once you are sure the new behavior has become a habit, then move forward to the next.

2: Accountability

Both being accountable to yourself and having others keeping you honest can help drive the changes you want to see. This includes being able to have open and honest conversations about whether someone is displaying the desired new behavior or not, as well as constructive, meaningful conversations as to why not and how to improve. When we know others are going to be watching and are there to support us, it helps drive up the level of accountability we feel.

For example, when I was working on my communication habits and trying to make them more responsive rather than reactive, I involved my partner. Each day we discussed openly how my communications were going, what they could do to help me best develop the new behavior, and what I could try and do to improve. At the same time, they had chosen a committed action to work on that was just as personal, so the conversations were a part of a journey of growth for us both, together.

Not only did this drive me to be more aware of the action, but it became something I was naturally implementing. Throughout the day, I was constantly aware of the conversation coming later where we would ask "did I implement my action today?" Moreover, it also enabled a support mechanism. When changing behaviors, the support of others, leaders, and direct reports and/or coworkers, who are going through similar growth can offer tremendous comfort and enablement along the path to change.

3: Reflection

Hand-in-hand with accountability is reflection. You need to ask yourself every day, "did I engage the new behavior?" If not, "why not?" As you will then be able to see the trends and you can start making changes that can better help you make the behavior a norm. It is easy to simply say you will take committed actions, but without pausing to "check-in" you won't really see how well you are implementing them, nor are you able to change course as needed.

For example, when thinking about losing weight, I had once said to myself, "at work, I will eat a salad every day for lunch," as this would convert one meal into something nutritious. Following this, each day I would check in with myself, did I eat the salad for lunch? If not, why not? Then, with this information, I decided what I needed to do to make the behavioral change easier to attain. In this case, I started with the best of intentions, but my mornings were busy, and I quickly learned that I didn't have the time needed to prepare my salad each day, so I would just end up settling for something quick to grab. After a few days of reflection in which I realized I just wasn't doing the behavior, I reflected on why, what was my barrier? I realized it was the time aspect, so I decided to do meal prep on Sundays so that my salads could be thrown together really quickly in the morning. Reflecting daily on whether you implemented the new behavior, and looking at why you didn't, will allow you to continue the journey of growth with a better chance of success.

4: Forgiveness

It can be easy to fail at keeping a new behavior when you are trying to make that new habit an everyday act. During this time, more than ever, it takes the art of forgiveness--to forgive yourself in those moments in which you stumble and knowing it's ok to get right back up and try again, rather than continuing into the downward spiral.

When we think we have "messed up" it is easy to get stuck in a negative space or give up on the goal. However, in these moments, rather than correlating this one temporary action to the overall goal, it is better to reflect and forgive ourselves, then continue back on the right path straight away and make the changes needed. Forgiveness also extends to others. While others are trying to engage new, healthy, positive habits, forgiving them when they may slip up, will help keep them feeling supported through their journey. This not only goes for your family and friends, but your coworkers, your manager, and your leaders too.

Reading On...

Now, you will explore each of the 12 factors that contribute to people being able to perform and feel their best, what it means to individuals, teams, and organizations, as well as how they can manifest in behaviors. Each chapter will focus on a factor, how it can show up and explore its impact.

Along the way, there will also be valuable advice and life hacks for you as an individual, for managers, and organizational considerations, based on the practical application of our research and years of coaching people to perform and feel their best.

With that, let's get started!

The 12 Factors
For Cultivating Positively Energized, High Performance Workplaces and Lifestyles

CHAPTER ONE

Accountability

Holding oneself accountable for one's actions, mindset, behaviors and attitude.

In American football, there is saying: "Do your job." It's a strange mantra considering how team-focused the sport is. Football is said to be all about the spirit of companionship, and teamwork, and yet, its most important rule is one that in any other circumstance, would be perceived as utterly selfish and isolating. But that's because the sport of football understands something that fortune 500 companies struggle to succeed at every day.

Accountability is a true signifier of efficiency among teams. On the field, accountability at its best looks like 11 people moving as one unit almost as if they were performing a choreographed dance. At its worst, it looks like 11 people scrambling in all directions looking confused and yelling at one another as the other team blows by. It doesn't look much different in the workplace either. Similar to the workplace, a football team is composed of multiple players all assigned to specific roles and functions. They are solely responsible for that role and or function, because come game time, they need to know what to do and when to do it. If even just one player misses their assignment on a play the mistake can be costly. But, as the saying goes, we are all human and thus mistakes will arise. This mindset that football enforces, is that you're allowed to mess up--and your teammates will support you--but you need to be able to answer for that mistake. This subconsciously enforces the behavior of an accountable leader.

The level of accountability within your organization has a big impact on its overall levels of energy and productivity. Without high levels of accountability, organizations suffer. This causes employees to work in a flow of constant nervousness and fear instead of self-pride and success. The amount of distrust a lack of accountability creates can lead to major blockers on every level, and the further the problem is ignored the harder this blocker is to overcome. Problem-solving can become a marathon rather than a quick sit-down-and-fix. It may become hard to get to the root of internal issues because everyone is too busy trying to pass blame around and looking for sources beyond internal control. So how does one avoid such a costly energy blocker? Well, let's consider where accountability stems from.

The meaning is in the word. Accountability means you are accountable; you can literally be counted on. Others can trust that when you say you'll get something done, or when you make a commitment, you will see it through. On the surface, it means you'll make deadlines, you'll do what you say, and you will do all the tasks you commit to (even the smallest of tasks). This can be a hard trait to attribute to a whole team of people. Sure, you do your best to put together teams that can be counted on, but in an organization with plenty of moving parts and plenty of pieces required to complete the puzzle, a lot of issues could arise. That's why when you try to find people for your team, you search for those who are accountable on a deeper level.

When you are accountable others can trust that when you say you'll get something done, or when you make a commitment, you will see it through.

It is important to focus on the deeper character of an individual rather than the surface level of talent alone. In that search, you hope to find someone with a mindset that understands how to handle situations at the worst level, rather than just at the best. Someone who takes ownership over the outcome. It is only when things begin to fall apart, that one's accountability will begin to shine.

When something isn't working, or a problem occurs, an accountable individual will step up to the plate. First pointing out the problem, and openly accepting their role in the origin of the issue. A non-accountable individual might first want to avoid the problem or simply hope it'll go away. Once the problem is discovered their initial reaction might be one of self-justification or defensiveness. The issue with the latter is that this doesn't aid a team in solution creation. In fact, it only puts extra effort and requirements on everyone else to make up for the loss of time, money or even production value.

Imagine this scenario. An employee, Terry, is currently assigned to a big project in which he has to work with many different teams. He has to order something through the procurement system. When he goes to put through the order, he follows the process and notices that the estimated turnaround-time will be later than the date needed for the project. He looks up if there is an escalation process to expedite it. He discovers that the needs of his order do not comply with the escalation requirements. Fast forward a few weeks. In the project meeting, one of the milestones looks as if it may be missed. Because of the orders late arrival date, the activities of others will now be negatively impacted. In the call, the project manager tells Terry that if he had just let them know earlier, they could have seen what they could have done. Immediately, Terry is on the defensive and lets them know that he followed the process, did everything he could, and that there was no escalation opportunity.

People that do not take accountability often look for self-justifications or can react defensively.

What's the outcome? Well, Terry is annoyed and experiences negative emotions that distract him from what he needs to do. He thinks to himself, "I did all I could! I followed the process! It's not my fault if the process doesn't work?! This was not my issue; I did my job". As he thinks about it more and more, he gets more and more frustrated and annoyed, taking away concentration from the activities that actually needs to be done. He feels more disengaged from the project as he feels that the external factors are stopping him from being successful. On a personal level, Terry is actually putting himself at a huge disadvantage. His defensive and dismissive attitude create blockers that deny him key growth opportunities and the ability to provide additional value to his team. On the organizational level, the project manager and the rest of the team are a bit annoyed at Terry. They think how he messed up and how he didn't seem to care at all that there was something he could have done--such as tell them as soon as he realized the potential issue.

This could have gone very differently. Even if Terry failed to tell them earlier, when the project manager mentioned the issue in the meeting, Terry had an opportunity to take accountability. He could have apologized for the oversight of not telling them sooner, stated the facts (that he did look for an escalation path, but they didn't qualify), and then moved on to solutions. Both for the situation at hand and for lessons learned through the experience--for himself and the team. For example, the lesson learned here could have been that moving forward everyone should always flag potential issues as soon as they arise, allowing the team to then collectively discuss how they could work through the situation in the best way. Taking accountability would have kept the team in sync collectively and moving on to solutions would have shifted the mind-set to a more positive space. Instead, Terry's lack of ownership left him feeling frustrated and isolated, leading to numerous mental blocks.

That's why it's preferable to have accountable individuals on your team. Sure, they will still make mistakes, after all, there is a term human-error for a reason. However, at least they are able to accept their role and describe to you where in the process things went wrong. This creates a huge sigh of relief because your team is now better equipped to not only deal with a solution to the mistake but with the consequences that the mistake may have caused. There is also a chain of effects to having the accountable individual on your team versus the latter. An unaccountable team member can be viewed as a disease in some cases. Your team is probably already stressed as it is, and the last thing they need is someone lacking in accountability who is always jumping to excuses and searching for external reasons before even considering their role in an outcome. This can foster a larger feeling of resentment and negative emotions that, if left unattended, can spread, de-energizing the whole organization. In a team filled with highly accountable individuals, there is a sense of ease and trust among everyone. This allows each person to be able to focus on their work and the outcomes that they need to contribute to, without having to stress about who might be causing what and where. This is a key energizer to an efficient organization.

Of course, the presence of high accountability doesn't just appear out of nowhere. In fact, even if you hire the most accountable team, you can find there is still a chance of derailment. Because true accountability, like most things, stems from the top.

The culture and work environment your leaders curate for your teams will have the highest impact on how easy it is for your employees to function with an accountable mindset. This is especially true for your new hires and individual contributors as they are always trying to get a feel for the company culture and will emulate the behaviors they see. The easiest way for leadership to keep accountability encouraged and growing is to lead by example. Let's look back at the football analogy from earlier. Do you think a player is really going to step up and take the blame for a loss if they don't respect their coach? No, the coach came up with the game plan, the coach handed out the plays, why should the coach not be responsible when things go wrong? This type of thinking can be applied just as easily to the workplace, and it all depends on how your leaders decide to demonstrate accountability themselves. Even though the importance of accountability is clear, organizationally, research has shown a lack of accountability. In a Lee Hecht Harrison study, in partnership with HR People and Strategy, that included research across 21 industries and sectors and 33 global cities, they found that while 72% believed leadership accountability to be a critical business issue, only 37% were satisfied with the degree of accountability their leaders demonstrated in the USA, with the results being 71% and 31% globally.

Leaders have to role model accountable behaviors, holding themselves, and others, accountable.

Organizations that wish to foster accountability need to look closely at the behaviors of leadership. For example, leaders of teams must always first be able to analyze an issue and decide if it could have stemmed from a decision they made. Even if that decision played just the tiniest part in the outcome, then they need to be willing to account for that. Sometimes the link may not be direct. It could have been the hiring of a person or failing to enable an employee. A leader is there to put their teams in the best position to succeed, and failing to do so, at any level, is something they need to be able to seriously consider. Next, your leaders should have the ability to analyze how they handle certain situations. When something goes wrong, what's their initial reaction? How is their temperament? How do employees feel when discussing the issue with them? There needs to be a feeling of trust in communications. If an employee notices a mistake, they should feel comfortable discussing it with management knowing they won't suffer negative repercussions or a disrespectful response. This isn't possible if your leaders are known for passing blame or expressing frustration every time things get awry. A leader consumed in their negative emotions does not possess the ability to capably lead. No employee will feel comfortable speaking up when they don't even believe their opinions and words are being heard.

A leader should come into a bad situation with the mindset of wanting to discuss possible solutions. Think about your team for a second. When issues arise, do employees wish to discuss it openly with management and work together to find an issue? Are the individuals reflective on their role in the outcome? Or is the blame-game played? Blame is an easy bailout for those who struggle to accept responsibility and a frequent defense mechanism in organizations with a culture lacking in accountability. When there is a truly accountable culture, people own up to their role in a situation, they look to grow from experiences, and are not fearful of unnecessary negative consequences.

True accountability is the ability to hold yourself accountable for your actions, mindset, behaviors, and attitude. It is the understanding that you are in control of what you do and how you act. Frequently looking to external causes instead of analyzing our own role in outcomes can cause us to feel a lack of control in our own lives. Enabling this behavior can allow one to feel as if they've lost a grip on their life and leads to a never-ending feeling of internal dissatisfaction. It also hinders our ability to learn from these moments, which slows down our pace of growth.

People that demonstrate energizing behaviors tend to take authentic accountability for their behaviors. Being accountable means taking ownership over all outcomes, good or bad, because ultimately it means that no one else has control over us. When one comes to this realization, it can open the gates to the energizing mindsets necessary for true authenticity.

The difference is clear. In the hustle and bustle of a growing and fast-paced environment, it is important to check on your accountability levels. If they are low, find a solution, and if they're doing well, then find a way to keep growing. Your company can't afford to lose out on such a powerful energizer of success.

Tips and Advice

As individuals, it is important to be aware of the level of accountability we take. It is often far easier to look to external justifications than it can be to take a deeper look into our own actions. Justifying why we may have acted a certain way or made a certain decision is an easy habit to slip into. Listening out for when you use words like "but" or "because" and stopping to analyze those moments can open the door to meaningful growth. Circle back and focus on your actions, asking yourself--what could I have done differently? And, what can I learn from this? On the other hand, some people find themselves taking too much accountability, simply placing all the blame on themselves just to move past a difficult moment or quickly dismiss an uncomfortable conversation. Accurate accountability means you are able to draw the correct correlation between your actions, thoughts, and decisions to the outcome. When we do this, we can have the difficult conversations, move on to solutions, and experience pivotal learning moments. When coaching, we encourage people to find success partners to support them. These are people that care about you, that support you, and that can help hold you accountable in a loving, respectful way.

Another thing to remember is how to take accountability over progress in your personal life and for your own happiness. Asking yourself questions such as: What fulfills me? What makes me feel good? What do I need to feel valued? What do I want to do with my life? And, what makes me happy? Helps you to best invest your time and energy in the right way. Treating personal growth and goals with the same rigor as work objectives and goals increases progress. This can help you feel a greater sense of achievement, a feeling of worth, and supplies a fuel source of motivation.

As a manager, it is critical to demonstrate accountability and holding others accountable.

To demonstrate taking accountability over your own growth, you can ask for feedback. Asking your employees how you yourself may improve will encourage the behavior in others. As leaders, we often think we need to be perceived as fearless, invincible, or perfect. However, there is no such thing as perfect. If you say you are accountable, but your employees never see you apologizing or speaking about your role when something goes wrong, it works against building bonds of trust and authenticity. When something does not go as planned, maybe a goal is missed or something is late, it can be helpful to encourage open conversation. Start by talking about what you could have done differently and what you have learned. This sets the example and creates a safe space. Invite your employees to discuss their thoughts in one-on-ones by asking questions such as "what do you think you could have done?" as this can build comfort in taking accountability.

As an organization, a culture of accountability has to be fostered from the very top. This includes trustworthy leadership. Ask yourself, do your leaders hold themselves and each other accountable? Say sorry when they mess up? Take ownership over mistakes? And, do not play the blame game? To have accountability in your DNA, it is worth looking at your hiring practices too and seeing how you hire for accountability.

How it can show up

If you experience lower levels of accountability...

You may not be fully taking accountability for everything you want to do and achieve in life. Sometimes, we can find that we take accountability at work, but do not take accountability for making changes in our personal lives, or over actions that move us towards our personal goals.

It will help you to start practicing accountable behaviors. When a situation occurs, start taking a moment to think through why it happened? What did you do? What could you have done? Then, you can start taking the right actions to resolve the situation and move forward with a mindset of growth. It will also help to think about what you need to feel fulfilled, and to place accountability processes in motion, to create the plan and take the actions needed.

If your team or organization experiences lower levels of accountability...

It could mean that people are not feeling as though they have control over their outcomes. This can stem from experiencing external factors such as policy, process, or leadership having a negative influence over outcomes. However, it can also stem from a lack of correlation to the consequences of their own actions.

Sometimes, this can also indicate that the culture is somewhat fearful. Where people are scared to take accountability for outcomes should they not be positive or as desired.

The impact of this can be felt in an organization's performance. When people do not take accountability, it leads to wasted time spent on excuses and other actions, rather than moving forward to a solution for the issue. It also leads to feelings of discontent, as people can easily move into a state of "why bother?" when they perceive a lack of control over their lives and their ability to meet goals. An environment where people do not take accountability, and are not held accountable, can also foster higher levels of toxicity and stress.

CHAPTER TWO

Achievement

Embracing opportunities for growth and learning, setting challenging goals and acknowledging meaningful achievements.

The modern times of today leave us all in an endless flux of hustle-n-bustle. Trying to keep up with the perceived urgency of the professional world, increasing complexity, and unknown landscapes can lead to heightened pressure and anxiety. All of these stressors can cause increasingly overwhelming feelings leading to a loss of focus and clarity. The "always-on" pressure of our world is hard enough as is, without stopping to think about our total plate and all of life's responsibilities that come with it--all requiring our time and energy.

On an organizational level, when people are running from task to task, meeting to meeting, or putting out this fire and that, there is no time to pause, think, or reflect. There is no mental space to appreciate the efforts of others, nor the value they bring, which can create an energizer blocker that only aids in fostering further negative feelings and behaviors.

A sense of achievement is something that can be easily lost when trying to navigate the stress-filled maze of the workplace. Without the ability to acknowledge meaning through accomplishments it becomes harder to stay motivated, inspired, and encouraged by a sense of value. On every level, employees need to feel empowered by what they do and understand the meaning behind it. When these feelings begin to fade, productivity begins to linger. Understanding one's own accomplishments, personally and professionally, is an enabler for confidence and validation. It ignites a drive in us that fuels a mindset for growth, a hunger for success, and a desire to take on new challenges. The most effective organizations thrive off creating a sense of achievement within their workforce and find every opportunity to bring true meaning to those achievements.

> *Without the ability to acknowledge meaning through accomplishments it becomes harder to stay motivated and inspired.*

When a company fails to provide an overall feeling of accomplishment within their workforce, then employees will fail to see the meaning or value behind their successes and their work. It is not hard to see how this could be problematic.

These types of negative de-energizers can begin to link into a chain of blockers that can hold back an organization from ever achieving its full potential. A workforce unimpressed or unaware of the value in their work will never seek out opportunities for growth. They'll settle for doing the average day-to-day, not feeling the need to ever consider what goes on beyond their own tasks and responsibilities. Where they could be potentially seeking new opportunities to take on challenges, collaborating with and learning from other teams, or trying to achieve more within their own roles, they instead choose to go through the motions in a state of unmotivated "busyness."

Some organizations take note of these negative mindsets and still fail to properly form a countermeasure. In fact, some organizations even make it worse. Imagine this all too common scenario. An organization spots that a team or portion of their workforce seems to be underperforming in some areas. They take this lack of motivation, or uninspired work, to mean that the employee is not performing well or doesn't care. So, in an attempt just as uninspired as their employee's poor performance, they try to solve the problem with fear motivation, reminding them just how replaceable and expendable they could be if they don't step up their work. They place them on a review track with the hopes that this will get them back to a higher performance state. And sure, to some degree, this might provide said employee with a jolt of urgency to step up, but is that really supposed to last? The answer is no, and it's an answer that you won't have to wait long to discover on your own.

The issue with this approach is leadership not fully considering where this sudden dull in their workforce could be arising from. Usually, the types of leaders who find themselves in this dilemma are the ones who fail to realize that employees need a reminder of their achievements and a reminder to enjoy the meaning behind it. So, it also makes sense that they fail to realize that the employees may not be underperforming due to a lack of caring, but perhaps a lack of understanding the impact behind their work. This is not to say that people that are genuinely underperforming do not need a course of action, it is to say that it is worth really seeing where it is coming from.

Better would be to first start with leadership taking a moment to reflect on the current state of their workplace. This might require taking a quick pulse check to see where everyone is at. They need to be able to see if everyone, at all levels, has some idea of how their work provides value and is aligned to their own sense of purpose. They need to see if employees are using their strengths while working on something realistic and achievable that still challenges them at a pace that is sustainable. Once the values and purpose are understood, it's important to see if everyone understands how their work connects. Whether you have one person assigned to a specific task or a hundred people, the person with the task no one else has and the person with the task that 99 others have, should both feel the same level of value and validation. Employees should understand the very clear correlation between what they do and meaningful value. This is personal to each person. What is a meaningful accomplishment for one, is not the same for another. Nor is the mode of acknowledgement the same. It is all about finding out what works for your employees.

A sense of achievement goes beyond acknowledgement and understanding a correlation to value, it also comes down to some key behaviors and mindsets. For example, a curiosity to learn more or acquire new skills. These can be cultivated by exposing employees to new experiences. Setting achievable yet challenging goals for employees can instill a sense of accomplishment. The learning opportunity alone can go miles in granting a new perception of their progress. Oftentimes, our most challenging moments provide us with the greatest opportunities to shine. Those moments where you look back and remember, how when you started a project or started working on a goal, you had no idea how you would do it...but you did. People that tend to have higher levels of performance and fulfillment tend to take a moment to think about what they have achieved and the value it brought--to others, to their company, to themselves, and to the world. And, as a good manager, it is your duty to understand each employee's needs and capacity for challenge, as well as acknowledge the authentic moments of achievement--both individually and as a team. After all, when we celebrate our wins (our meaningful and authentic wins), it reinforces our strengths and brings out the behaviors we want to show up and keep at the forefront.

Tips and Advice

Our achievements and the meaning we find from them can be as unique to us as our favorite reading spot on a rainy morning. It could be a personal win, overcoming a challenge, an award or a promotion. It is something that you have attained, something you have done that makes you feel good, and provides the sense that you are progressing towards your desired future. Achievements are not solely those massive outcomes that your organization considers a huge win. Perhaps, you are just proud of a presentation you created today. Taking the time to celebrate the smaller wins keeps up levels of positivity and motivation. Try setting aside a couple of minutes to think to yourself, what did you feel good about today? Or this week?

It is also important to look at accomplishment within your personal life. If you feel that work is great and that you are giving your all, but things are slipping in your personal life, it can feel like a lack of accomplishment. It starts with the question, are you feeling fulfilled? If not, then look at what you need to do, or how best to pivot so that you may start feeling this way. Look at how you can spend just a little time on the things that make you feel good. Perhaps it is spending time on a hobby, something you are passionate about, or learning a new skill. It can help to set goals that are realistic and achievable. For example, if you set a goal to lose 10 pounds at the end of the month, but your lifestyle includes a lot of eating out, this may not be too attainable, and you will be left disappointed and unmotivated. This can ultimately leave a bad taste in your mouth when it comes to goal setting as a whole and cause you to give up on the idea altogether. It is more realistic to say, I'll go to the gym 10 times this month. If you go more times, then you met and exceeded your goals, but more importantly you are left excited and motivated to accomplish the next task.

Managers that feel good about themselves and feel as though they are moving forward, have a contagious positive energy that employees can feel. Sharing and celebrating wins with your team creates a positive mental space. It is easy to focus on what needs to be done or get caught up in the task-list, however, it is important to discuss what is going well with your team. From here, people are more open to collaboration, to growth opportunities, to risk, and are more comfortable with change. As a manger, ask yourself if you are taking the time to acknowledge your employees and take pride in the advancements they have made towards their goals. It is important to do this based on the individual and their preferences. Some may like more public acknowledgement, some may not. It is also about taking the time to understand your employees' personal and professional desires, and then creating and aligning their goals in a way that challenges them, but is achievable, so that they can progress towards them. Looking at your employees' strengths and areas for enhancement, and then looking at options to support them, such as partnering with a peer or exposing them to tailored opportunities, can also help them feel as though they are progressing.

As an organization, do you have the tools and supporting structures in place to enable people to feel valued? This could be ways to give kudos and praise, managers who can communicate authentic acknowledgement, a reward system, or simply sharing stories. This should be based on what resonates with your employees, and what makes them feel valued, as one size does not fit all.

How it can show up

If you experience a lower level of achievement...

It is likely that you are not feeling that your value is being exposed or recognized. You may feel stuck in a rut or as though you could do more. It can help to really think about what a genuine accomplishment is for you.

Then, when you do achieve something, take the time to acknowledge it by thinking about what you have done and how it provided a positive impact to someone else, to a goal, or an outcome. It can help to start acknowledging your accomplishments yourself as well as sharing them with those close to you.

If your team or organization experiences lower levels of achievement...

It could mean that people are not correlating their genuine accomplishments by seeing the line between their actions and efforts, to meaningful, valuable outcomes.

It could also indicate that there is a lack of continuous growth opportunities or a lack of capacity to actually take the time to reflect, acknowledge accomplishments, or develop. When a culture fosters a nature of jumping from task-to-task, with little time to reflect on the wins, it loses out on moments that can foster contagious positive emotions and higher levels of team-esteem.

This can impact how fulfilled your employees feel. Making valuable contributions from our skills, strengths, and from who we are as a person promotes positive emotions. When we do not feel as though we are achieving and growing, it is easy to just go through the motions, which leads to higher levels of disengagement.

CHAPTER THREE

Alignment of Time

Correlating time, energy, and efforts to one's purpose, skills, and to what is meaningful.

As mentioned, the world can sometimes fill us with a sense of urgency, and it can feel as if the time in the day is beginning to shrink. There are only 24 hours in a day. This is not something we can change, no matter who we are or how much money we have. But how those hours are spent is the most critical differentiator between highly energized people and organizations, and those that tend to feel more overwhelmed, stressed, and de-energized.

In our always-on world, with emails arriving at all times, the ability to check in to various project management tools at a moment's notice, and the constant streams of information being shoved in front of us, it is no wonder that we are increasingly distracted, tired, and why the standard answer to "how are you?" tends to be, "busy, but good."

We all have responsibilities. We have work responsibilities and responsibilities to ourselves and others. When our work responsibilities pile up, oftentimes we find it easier to sacrifice the time we spend on ourselves or we cut short our non-work-related activities. We have all been there. That deadline comes up, so we cancel a dinner date with a friend, or that email comes in, so we are distracted instead of focused on the conversation at hand with our partner or relative. However, people that demonstrate higher levels of engagement in life, and at work, tend to be aware and sensitive to how they spend their time. They take actions to create and respect boundaries that enable them to correlate their time to their purpose, skills, and to activities that are meaningful to them. In fact, the Harvard Business School conducted a survey with 4,000 executives worldwide and found that the most successful leaders consciously managed their time and priorities to maximize their professional and personal lives. By consciously utilizing time in this way, they can maximize moments of peak clarity and focus and increase capacity to make time for work, play, and the people that matter.

> *People that demonstrate higher levels of engagement in life, and at work, take actions to create and respect boundaries that enable them to correlate their time to their purpose, skills, and to activities that are meaningful to them.*

The problem most commonly occurs when we first begin our careers. We think the formula to success is simple, work harder and longer than anyone else and we'll be the first name that comes to mind when talks of promotions arise. But the truth is longer hours do not equate to stronger performance. Erin Reid, a professor at Boston University's Questrom School of Business, conducted a study on long work hours with a top strategy consultant firm. In her study, she was unable to find any evidence of a difference in the work done between employees who worked for 80 hours, and those who simply pretended to. When it comes to the age-old battle of quality vs quantity this is a clear won battle.

Think of the remarkable stories and legends of protagonists determined to achieve all their desires. These age-old tales were probably so inspiring due to the determination and strong-willed nature of the leading character. But, as most great stories go, these thrilling characters most likely did not come without their flaws. Whether it's Achilles leaping into as many wars as he can in search of glory, or Captain Ahab dedicating his life to a reclusive hunt, eventually everyone wears down and can lose sight. Seeking to fast track our way into glory with a relentless schedule will only lead to a noble yet futile downfall.

While it may be easy to simply say long hours are bad, there have been numerous studies to back up the negative truths of an overly devoted work schedule. Perhaps the first to consider is the negative toll it may take on an employee's health and how that may lead to a worse bottom line for an organization as a whole. Back in March 2017, the Australian National University published the results to their study on the number of hours an average an employee should work. After testing a collection of over 8,000 candidates the study concluded that, on average, the work limit should be set at 39 hours per week, as that is the point when performance drops begin to happen, and mental states begin to collapse. Huong Dinh, one of the researchers on the study, concluded that "long work hours erode a person's mental and physical health, because it leaves less time to eat well and look after themselves properly." The study even went on to include that working past our limits could lead to impaired sleep, depression, heavy drinking, diabetes, impaired memory, and heart disease. Now, obviously no one needs to point out the unfortunate effects of dealing with such health risks, but for an organization worried about how this might hurt their bottom line, this could mean an increase in health insurance and loss of effective performance which is easily translated into a dent in the profit margins. While the number of hours we work ebbs and flows, dependent on many things, the study serves to highlight the importance of work-life harmony.

When you continuously overwork, you begin to lose out on time that could be spent elsewhere. Your life slowly begins to revolve more round work and you slowly lose sight of what you're even working for. This tunneled focus can create a lack of feeling value in not only life or work, but in oneself. When we lose that sense of value and motivation our engine begins leaking fuel, and we all know that pushing the car that extra hour down the road with the gas tank on empty never works the way we hoped. This is why it is imperative that as individuals, and organizations, we set time for mental and emotional maintenance. Social psychologist Ron Friedman is no stranger to this. Friedman notes that leaders who overwork themselves with long hours cause an expectation that their team members can never fully disconnect from their work. He speculates that this can lead to employees feeling less engaged with their jobs and drains them of their emotional energy.

It is important that employees understand they need to take the time to disconnect and that the organization supports this culture. How employees choose to set their schedule and work their hours can be heavily influenced by the company they're doing it for. Let's return to what Friedman said earlier, about how leaders can set this expectation for their team members. Organizations can subconsciously encourage over working hours and a work-first mindset. Organizations with more energized employees tend to manage by objectives rather than the number of hours, or the length of time, someone is "available." Placing a focus on the value, contributions, and goals achieved, rather than exactly where or how an employee works, promotes a sense of autonomy over time which has been found to foster positive emotions.

Another way organizations can help support their employees is by understanding their strengths and desires--which activities and types of work energizes them? Do they like creative work, collaborating with people, or more focused work? Aligning their efforts to the kinds of activities that energize them evokes higher levels of engagement and productivity.

And lastly, being aware. Both as individuals and from an organization's perspective, being aware of how time is used, and creating harmony between professional and personal responsibilities, will enable each person to focus on their own wellbeing, their relationships, and their work in the best way for them. Being aware of your personal energy patterns, when you feel more alert or tired throughout the day, and your body's signals, can help you better plan different types of tasks at different times. For example, if you concentrate best in the morning, then you can plan for tasks that require dedicated concentration in those hours. This can help you use your 24 hours more effectively.

After all, every employee needs to spend time on their own self-care, nurturing relationships that matter, helping others, and professional achievements. When time is used wisely, and task and time align, energy is spent in the best way.

Tips and Advice

Individually, this means looking at how you are spending your time. Each of us needs to spend time and energy on our own self-care, work, and with others. It is about looking at how you can make space for these, in a way that best fits your needs. You can start by looking at how you spend your time today. This can help you find easy shifts that open up and enhance your capacity, as well as how you can use your time in the best way. How you use your 24 hours can dramatically increase your productivity, value, and impact. For example, think about when you feel more alert, or tired, and then try to plan activities around that so that you can best focus or be creative.

When aligning your time, to be effective, you will need to do some things and not do some things. This will start with awareness and then be about making decisions about your boundaries that will protect your time and energy. For example, with meetings, think about how vital it is for you to be there? Can the collaboration be done in a way that makes better use of your time? Can it be shorter? When you are clear on your boundaries, it becomes easier to have conversations about why you can or cannot do something. A good place to start, is writing down the things that energize you, make you feel happy, are priorities, and what you are good at. Then you can start to see how to shift your time to do more of what makes you feel good. When we take the lead with our energizing activities, we are more confident and we are easier to work with as we exude positive energy.

For managers, it is important that employees are leveraging their strengths, but also being challenged and are growing. For some employees it can be applying their strengths to new projects or challenges, for some it can mean learning new skills. You want to make sure they are investing some of their time on experiences and activities that provide them with the sense that they are growing to the next stage on their desired journey. You can help your organization and employees by building realistic goals that they can build momentum from. Here, you must understand the people on your team, who needs what to work in the most effective way, and then work with their process.

Organizationally, it is important that leaders model the behaviors they want to cultivate in the organization. For example, if as a company, you tout work-life balance, but leaders are sending out emails at 10:30pm or 1am, then employees will not see exemplifying behaviors to match the philosophy. It is also about empowering your people to make decisions that impact their work and life, understanding their workstyle, how they work best, and affording them the flexibility to work in ways that best suit them. You can think about how you incorporate flexibility, how you accommodate workstyles, and which technologies and tools support these workstyles.

How it can show up

If you experience lower levels of alignment in task and time...

It is likely that your time ratios are off. You may not be spending enough time nurturing the relationships that matter, helping others, or on yourself when it comes to enjoying healthy activities and quiet, reflective time. It can help to take stock of how you are spending your time so that you can best shift your ratios. You may want to begin with a time journal. Simply logging how you are spending your time and energy each hour, for a week or two, will highlight patterns where you can make shifts that allow you to use your time more wisely.

If your team or organization experiences lower levels of alignment in task and time...

It could mean that people are not spending time on activities that energize them. This may include not being able to use their strengths enough or seeing how they provide value.

It could also indicate that people have a pace of work that is unsustainable. Perhaps there are always fires to put out, there is a lack of focus, or a lack of direction and priorities. It is unlikely that they are finding the time to take care of themselves, nurture relationships that matter to them, or be present in other parts of their lives, due to the time spent on work efforts (including tasks, meetings, and thinking about work).

This can impact their wellbeing in several ways. When work gets in the way of life responsibilities, it can evoke negative emotions and lead to higher levels of stress, burnout, and lower levels of productivity.

CHAPTER FOUR

Authenticity

Acting with compassion, being genuine, and living one's values.

Authenticity is the foundation of core habits for all successful and energized leaders. Think of it as the Swiss Army Knife of successful mindsets. When people live life at truly authentic levels they stand out and tend to be admired for it. This habit works as a guiding compass for all things, so that when we get lost or begin to fall off our path, we always know how to find our way back. It can be hard to make this a daily behavior due to the pressures, stress and anxiety we feel from society, as well as our personal and our professional worlds. Sometimes, we may think it's simply better to fit in, mimic the behavior of others, or keep quiet rather than speak our minds. However, those who truly desire success in life, know what it takes to get there, and they know that they need to experience congruence between the behaviors they portray and their personal value system.

Authenticity is all about being true and faithful to yourself. It means you are comfortable in demonstrating what you stand for and consistently display your core values through your actions. It means that even when things get tough, you are mindful of others and treat them with compassion. It means you are open. Open to the thoughts and perspectives of others, even when they may differ from own. To be authentic, you need to understand a lot about yourself first. You have to know the set of values that you stand by, you need to understand how your moral compass works, and you need to be faithful to your principles and opinions without feeling threatened by the thoughts of others.

It's not always simple in a society where we can easily feel pressured to follow the example set by others to succeed. But the truth is, even though we can learn from the successes of others, we still have to be authentic, because those people didn't succeed without being true to themselves. Steve Jobs had a lot of ideas that no one wanted to believe in, JK Rowling had a story that over 100 agencies thought no one wanted to read, and even Oprah had to deal with her fair share of naysayers. But every hero and historical harbinger of success had to decide at one point, to either compromise their ideals to fit in a little more or stick true to what they knew would work and show the world something amazing. History has shown which choice was the favored one.

Authenticity is all about being true to yourself, being comfortable with yourself and what you stand for, and demonstrating your core values through your actions.

It is one of those mindsets that may seem like some people are born with it already embedded into their system. But that doesn't mean it's not attainable for those who don't find it so easy to achieve.

Attaining a true authenticity all comes back to how you define yourself. If you can't tell yourself, on a daily basis, what your core values are, then you might find it hard to live life by your own compass. That's ok though, just because you can't say it aloud it doesn't mean that your core values aren't there. Try thinking of what values bring you joy in some way. Think about a friend you admire, a favorite actor you love to watch, or even your favorite characters on a show, and ask yourself what values you really respect in them that draws you to them. It could be their ability to stand up to anyone, or maybe they're humble and down to earth and show respect to everyone they come across. The things you respect or enjoy in others says a lot about your internal compass and what you value most. You could even consider your childhood and think of the adults you watched growing up. What made you look up to them? Whether it was a teacher, a coach, or a family member. All these things work towards shaping your value system even if you don't recognize it.

Keep in mind, being authentic doesn't mean you have to be the most well-spoken person in the room, the loudest in the room, or the first to voice your opinion. Try starting from a place of compassion, in every situation. You want people to feel heard around you, you want them to feel as though their thoughts or opinions are listened to. You want others to feel comfortable around you. Being kind and open with others creates a feeling that only true, authentic leaders can really grant, and it's powerful once done right. Be a helping hand, be an ear to others, and they'll respect you and begin reciprocating the feeling.

It can also help you to think back to times in which you have experienced being angry with someone or experienced guilt about your behaviors. Sometimes the causes of these emotions are indicators that we, or someone else, offended our value system. When we behave in a way that is not congruent to our values, we can feel badly about it. When someone else behaves in a way that contradicts our values, we can feel angry or upset. That's why thinking about who you want to be (rather than always focusing on what you want to do), can help you build a solid foundation.

Unfortunately, the sad truth of the business world is that many great future leaders are lost due to their inability to reach authenticity. Many factors play a role in this. Sometimes, this can stem from feeling they have to behave a certain way for a promotion, sometimes, they are coming from a place of fear, but sometimes, it's due to the very fabric of the organization. When the organization's cultural values are misaligned with that of employees, it can foster negative emotions. When an organization says on paper what it stands for, and then behaviors and actions differ from that, it causes a feeling of incongruence.

The problem also occurs when organizations and companies don't properly entice these mindsets amongst their workforce. Sometimes the culture around workers, especially at lower levels, is one that says, 'do what you're told and fit in where you belong.' Which completely undercuts evoking any feeling of working to your best capabilities and doing what you can to help the organization succeed.

Think about this scenario. A company realizes that they have been experiencing lower levels of employee engagement for a few years now. They are finding it challenging to retain talent and realize that their organization's culture needs to be revamped to better engage and attract long-term talent, allowing them to better serve their customers. A team is formed to tackle this project. They work to make sure that the organization's cultural values are defined and established. One of which is around inclusion--that every employee feels comfortable to share their perspective. In the following months, there is a series of presentations and coffee-talks, as well as wall art describing their values around the office, all to ensure that the company values are well communicated to the whole employee base. In a year's time, they conduct another employee engagement survey. The results are similar and there has been no real sustained change. Analyzing the results, they discover that employees do not feel comfortable sharing their perspectives. The leadership team is left stumped. They had made clear investments in creating their value system and communicating it to employees so that everyone was aware of it. Sound familiar?

Let's look at how that could have gone...While the first step was taken to determine their values, when you want to live the values, the journey does not end there. What happened was that the behaviors necessary to demonstrate their values were not fully cultivated. To live their value of inclusion, where everyone feels comfortable to share their perspective, management, cross-functional teams, and leadership, all have to understand how to respond to feedback, really listen to it, digest it, and make it feel represented in an environment in which all perspectives are authentically valued. This includes not just making sure the behaviors and mindsets are cultivated, but also hiring for the various behaviors that align to the values. Living their values authentically would have taken time to engage new behaviors, however, with a purposefully planned effort, this would have led to a sustained positive impact.

Values have to be demonstrated clearly through actions, not just be something that is written down or spoken about.

When values become a checkbox item, or just something that is only communicated rather than demonstrated through behaviors, we lose the real impact they can bring. When employees feel in alignment with the organizational values, they feel more positively and are more engaged.

When businesses don't encourage the feeling of individuality and self-worth among employees they begin to lose out on many aspects of future leadership. Even the leaders they do groom will rise in the company with a restrained feeling. This can be especially true when it comes to diversity in the workplace. It has been found that minorities and female workers tend to feel more of a pressure to fit in, prove themselves, or be a certain way to progress. The confidence gap between them and the majority is wide and further encourages them to stay tucked in the background. This could cost your company some great future leaders. Today's climate can make it difficult considering the sense of political tension and even sometimes religious stigmas. But being authentic has nothing to do with forcing your beliefs or ideals on others, and neither should it be when it comes to encouraging authenticity.

A research study done by Ethan R. Burris from McCombs School of Business set out to see the true effect of leadership having an open speaking environment with subordinates. They studied 7,578 subordinates and 355 general managers within a national restaurant chain. Their findings discovered that agreement and openness between employees and managers lead to more favorable outcomes. The study went on to discover that managers who were encouraging of employee ideas and opinions reduced employee turnover by 32 percent, saving the business at least $1.6 million a year. These kinds of results speak for themselves and make it undeniable that organizations who fail to encourage a culture of authenticity are losing out on major gains from it.

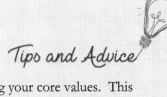

Tips and Advice

Living authentically is linked to knowing your core values. This includes looking at what is most important to you and defining your non-negotiables. When we know our non-negotiables, with our own behavior, with work, and with our relationships, it puts everything into perspective. Asking yourself questions such as, which traits do you respect and admire in others? Which traits do you dislike in others? And, what do you want to be known for? Can help you define your core values. These values can then act as a guide, keeping you true in your decision making and how you respond to all situations. Your values are the foundation to your success. Then, in the workplace, if you find yourself in a role or environment where your values are not met, they get lost, or they are not supported, you can decide your best next step. Do you need to make shifts? Do you need to move on? Do you need to include a hobby or project in your life to add value to what may be missing from your work life?

Authenticity is also being mindful of others and responding from a place of empathy. When someone does something, or is acting a certain way, take a moment to think before reacting. What may be causing them to act this way? We have all behaved in a way, at some point in our lives, which may be less than ideal or desired. Remembering these moments can help you treat others with compassion. Shifting your perspective in these moments and remembering similar times in which you have felt a similar way can help. For example, if someone is stressed and snaps at you, think about the times when you have been stressed and were snappy so that you can better understand where may be coming from.

For managers, it is important to role model living their values. For example, if a manager says they are open, appreciative of others' perspectives, and asks for feedback, but then has no time to listen to concerns or does not provide employees with the sense that they were heard, this leads to a conflicting workplace culture. It is also important that managers respond from a place of compassion. In moments when someone is underperforming or perhaps misses an objective, asking questions such as, "are you ok?" Or, "what's going on?" Can help keep an open mind and encourage meaningful reflection. Understanding each employee's personal values can support healthy communications. Remembering that not everyone functions or drives themselves in the same way, it is important to be cognizant of what each person responds to and their value system.

Organizationally, it creates healthier workplaces when leaders practice the values with their team. What are the cultural values? Are they demonstrated? It is important that people are supported for who they are, and that employees feel they are in a place where they can express themselves naturally, without judgement or bias. Actively fostering the growth of such an environment, means taking a look at policies and procedures. For example, when hiring, how do you remove bias? Do you look at values? You may find a candidate that clearly meets objectives, however if their way of doing so or behaviors are not aligned to the values, it can lead to a toxic environment.

How it can show up

If you experience a lower level of authenticity...

It is likely that you are having some conflict with what your values are. If you know what your values are, then you may be experiencing a state of incongruence between your value system and either your behaviors, your relationships with others, or what you are spending time doing.

It can be useful to start thinking about situations in which you felt you could not, or did not, behave how you wanted to or say what you wanted to. Why didn't you? How did you feel? Exploring why you feel certain ways can help you identify what is really holding you back.

It can also help to reflect upon what your values are and why they may be in conflict--as this can cause us to feel guilt, anger, frustration, or sadness. Looking at when you felt bad, and exploring what was going on at that time, will help you see what you need to do in the future.

If your team or organization experiences a lower level of authenticity...

You likely are experiencing a state of incongruence between your organization's cultural values and how they are manifesting through behaviors. Employees may not be exhibiting actions that align to the cultural values or they may not be seeing these behaviors role modeled by leadership. Oftentimes, this stems from a lack of openness to the perspectives of others or a lack of authentic appreciation for diversity of thought--especially those that may differ to one's own.

Sometimes, this can also be an indication that the culture is one in which people demonstrate negative behaviors in challenging, frustrating, or stressful times--which can have a compounding effect on the organization as a whole.

The impact of this can be felt in the very energy of the organization and in the level of employee engagement. It can help to look at defining your cultural values, and how you are fostering an environment in which the behaviors, at all levels, are clearly being demonstrated.

CHAPTER FIVE

Awareness

Being aware of oneself, others, and one's environment.

We are constantly surrounded by signs in our everyday interactions.
Some come as warnings, some shine the light on opportunities, and others
are simply there to provide better insight into how best to respond. But
these cues, as numerous as they can be, don't amount to much if we are
not aware enough to spot them or take the time to think about what they
mean to us. Positively energized people are able to digest all these social
cues, and hints from their surroundings, and use them as a guide that
helps them through all situations in the best way. But that kind of
awareness isn't always so easy to practice or make the norm. It takes work
and continues to grow.

Unfortunately, while we should be open and aware of the indicators in
our lives, it tends to be the distractions of life that absorb the majority of
our focus. When we lose our focus, we can lose our ability to be aware.
These indicators help us understand how to handle situations, how to
avoid mental blockers, and how to seize energizing opportunities. These

signals can come in numerous fashions, whether it be physical or mental, from the actions of others, or from something in our environment. The more receptive we are to them, the more we can be purposeful in our responses, take the right actions to be happier and healthier, and change course if needed. It's about understanding how you function in different settings or situations, understanding how your body feels, and understanding what different emotions may signify.

An awareness of yourself, your responses, and external stimulus can even help you see an issue arising before it arrives. This could provide an opportunity to create a solution before the problem actually occurs or escalates. Being aware gives you the time to begin to prepare and decide on any countermeasures. For example, when you are aware of the signs of an emotional response, you can put into place a response system to handle the moment, so that you can later respond in a better way without unintended consequences or guilt over an impulsive behavior. When we do not understand our triggers, signals, or the perspective of others it can lead to explosive reactions, reactive decision making, and defensive stances. What could just be a simple talk-it-out and find a solution issue, could drag out into a bridge-burning snap decision. Those making sure to work on their awareness and keep up a receptive attitude don't have to worry about such regretful moments.

Being aware of your emotions, your triggers, external stressors, the perspectives of others, and context, helps ensure the best response to any situation.

Those more receptive can take time to fully digest any situation while still adapting to what may be coming next. That's what is so vital about an energized awareness. You don't only stay alert to the happenings around you, but it keeps sudden shifts or changes in setting from throwing you for a curve. In the world of high-pressure business, uncertainty, and always-on stress, this can be the difference between closing that giant deal or walking away with a disappointing outcome.

Your level of awareness influences your ability to strategize. To understand what is happening around you and be able to pause and formulate what to do next. At its best, it allows you to plan out your moves, be prepared for different outcomes, and logically take the best course of action with the information at hand. At its worst, you're left in a storm of confusion and stress, normally feeling some level of guilt or disappointment over the course of actions taken. But high alert awareness isn't just about noticing your own personal indicators.

Those around you are constantly giving off their own signals and indicators, whether they may be aware of them or not. If you can take into account the clues coming from all around you, even those coming from others, you will more easily connect with people and read them as you navigate through conversations. Two people both with high levels of awareness may find themselves working together to handle situations, even if they're not verbally communicating. This allows for better chemistry and teamwork resulting in a more energized organization able to function at higher levels. This is a sign of a great leader, someone aware of their own clues but still keeping an eye out for the indicators of others.

This ability allows leaders to best serve their employees. For example, understanding when others need to be left alone or need to be checked on. In fact, studies published in Emotion and Mindfulness found that more self-aware people demonstrated greater cognitive empathy. Empathy has long been associated with better relationships and leadership, as the ability to understand others leads to a greater ability to support them, bond with them, and cultivate trust.

So, being aware of yourself, other's behaviors and perspectives, and your environment will allow you to take a step back, pause, and formulate the best course of action for your goals, your wellbeing, and your relationships. Beyond this, it enables you to grow. As when we are self-aware and reflective, we can see opportunities for growth, we can better understand our strengths, feel connected to what energizes us, and have a clear line of sight to our areas of weakness.

Being aware of how other people may affect us also becomes an important part of awareness. There are people that drain your energy and those that lift you up. We cannot always choose who we work with, however, we can set boundaries that help us manage our interactions and ensure we can re-energize ourselves after interacting with them.

Tips and Advice

As individuals, our response systems are built on our beliefs, emotions, and experiences. We may have experienced things in our lives, stemming back to childhood, which can cause us to react in certain ways in our current life. Perhaps you had a parent who never acknowledged your achievements. You may now find it difficult to acknowledge your own achievements or even react to others praise by minimizing your effort or contribution. Perhaps you experienced something that caused you to develop defensive or reactive habits that are impacting your life, relationships, or work. Becoming aware of your triggers and emotions, helps you build healthy, positive, and productive response systems. When we react to an event impulsively, with passive-aggressiveness or extreme anger, we usually are not giving much thought to what we are saying and how we are acting. This tends to occur when we do not fully resolve a past issue, do not see different perspectives, our value system is offended, or we don't get something we want. It is better, when you find yourself in a situation, to first acknowledge your emotions, assess the facts, process it, and acquire perspective. Then, considering the context of the situation and best desired outcome, you can decide the best approach to handle it. This is responding, rather than reacting.

It is all about reflecting and realizing. You can look back at different situations you have been in to analyze what evoked various emotions, such as anger, frustration, or sadness. Often, we feel a physical clue. For example, perhaps when you feel angry you may feel some tension or the sensation of "blood-boiling". Becoming aware of these can help you create better responses in these moments, as understanding your own feelings will help you decipher if it is a person or the trigger that is currently setting you off. You can find language that you are comfortable with, that you can have on hand to use in these moments, while you work on creating better automatic response systems. Like in moments of anger, maybe you need to take a moment to collect your thoughts, then find the language of communication you are most comfortable with before reacting.

For managers, it is about demonstrating awareness of themselves and being aware of their employees. Being aware of employees' feelings and triggers will strengthen communications and increase collaboration. When communicating feedback, be aware of how your employee receives information, their communication style, and make sure you are specific in providing information that helps them move forward. Not just saying, "your presentation could have been better." But, providing details around how it could have been and what they can do to improve their skills. It is important for managers to be aware of how others perceive them, not just how they perceive themselves. Sometimes, with the best of intentions, we can take actions which affect people in ways that we don't even know. Asking for open and candid feedback about yourself, your behaviors, and how to improve, all work towards building that awareness muscle. Lastly, many managers can be afraid to say I don't know, or I'm sorry, or in worse cases they may blame others or their team. Role modeling self-awareness, that it is ok not to know something, taking accountability, and collaborating, can encourage employees to also be reflective and more self-aware.

Organizationally, it is important to be aware of how several aspects of a culture impact employees' ability to get their work done, grow, and feel good. Understanding the impact of things such as tools, space, and communications, will help you make better decisions. Often, an undesired outcome can occur, or a reactive decision made. At this level, being able to take accountability and say sorry demonstrates that an organization is aware of their decisions, their role and the impact on employees. Better yet, is taking pause to look at the options, context of a situation, and the goal, which allows a more purposeful response that produces the best possible outcome. While many leaders think they are self-aware, a large study in the Journal of Clinical and Social Psychology found that only 10-15% are actually as aware as they think. It is important to ask yourself, how are you helping your employees to become more self-aware? How are you providing them opportunities to accurately know how they are doing, learn their strengths, areas for enhancement, or impact of their behaviors?

How it can show up

If you experience a lower level of awareness...

It is likely that you may not be fully aware of your emotions, feelings, and body signals so that you can respond in the best way. It can help to take time to notice and acknowledge how you are feeling at several times, in different scenarios, and what your triggers may be for certain emotions.

Awareness is a critical piece of maintaining a positive mental state. The more aware you are of your feelings, context, and of others, the better you will be able to grow a healthy response system.

If your team or organization experiences lower levels of awareness...

It could mean that you have people that are unable to be fully aware of a situation, their role or contribution to an outcome. They may not be able to communicate with clarity as they may not be aware of how best to do so. This can impact the levels of accountability in the team and hinder growth and development. It can also reduce the level of connectedness the team feels, as people may not be able to interact in the best way for themselves and others.

Additionally, it could indicate that they lack the ability to analyze situations to make the right comparisons and determine the best action given the information. Combined with the likelihood that they are not as purposefully responsive as they could be, this can lead to a more reactive environment and suboptimal decision making.

CHAPTER SIX

Basic Wellbeing

Ensuring that basic needs around health and wellbeing are taken care of as well as practicing kindness to oneself and others.

This is a big one. A lot of how you keep your basic energy levels up and going often comes down to your ability to stay on top of this one area. You can't commit to excellence in your work if you can't commit to excellence in your own self-care. Unfortunately, the little things often get lost when it comes to self-care. We constantly sacrifice these things in a race for time and reserved effort. We do a daily dance trying to make bargains with ourselves about what is necessary and what can be missed. We say to ourselves, oh we'll just pick up a quick meal today from the drive-thru and make it up with an extra walk this weekend. We think, well maybe it's ok to stay up an extra hour or two to finish some work tonight, because this Saturday we'll get to sleep in. But Saturday is still three days away and that extra walk won't seem so appealing when we just want to sleep.

The truth is plain and simple. Those crunch time moments will always find a way to sneak up on us, but constantly sacrificing elements of self-care is not strategizing, it's simply entering into a lose-lose bargain with your physical, mental, and emotional wellbeing. Sure, an extra set aside time for rest will be good for later, but you're still sacrificing what you need to make it through the now. Sometimes, when we get caught in the whirlwind that is life's constant chores and responsibilities, we forget to really consider the wear and tear we do to ourselves. A great work ethic and resilient demeanor are great, but there needs to be a balance. Sure, Kobe would hit the gym at five in the morning for a workout, but he also knew that instead of doing laps until midnight he should probably take an ice bath before the next game. Hemingway would spend days revising each paragraph of his novels ten times, but he still understood that his work was nothing if he didn't go out and enjoy the world. The greats understand something. They know that, though there is a greatness inside us ready to be tapped into, it will mean nothing without proper care and management.

There are two pressing sides of wellbeing and self-care to consider. There is the more glaringly obvious side to it--the exterior physical maintenance. This is the stuff we're taught all our lives: three square meals a day, 7-8 hours of sleep, a weekly dose of exercise, make sure you eat your greens etc... And, while over time science and studies have revealed more about what truly goes into proper health management, the importance is still the same. We need to take care of our bodies to function properly.

Then, there is the second side, that not so in-your-face side. And, most often the side we forget to consider--the interior maintenance, the mental, spiritual, and emotional maintenance. This means taking the time to do mental checks and checking in with yourself. Reminding yourself to not be so harsh and critical over your flaws or mistakes. You need to make sure you're not bringing yourself down too much because you need to be able to bounce back on track when things begin to get tough. If you're not taking the time to make sure you're being kind to yourself, then the hits you take end up landing even harder. How we manage our mental health determines our outlook and mindsets for dealing with all of life's challenges. It has been found that self-compassion is correlated to success because it supports self-acceptance and improvement. A 2011 study, conducted by the University of California, found that self-compassion can increase our motivation to recover from failure as well as increase our motivation to improve ourselves.

It is not hard to see how heavy the impact can be to an organization when employees begin to lose concern over their wellbeing, or when an organization does not support and foster a culture of wellbeing. In fact, peoples' energy levels, expressions, and work performance will directly reflect it. Even the little things can build up. For example, the longer-term impact of sitting all day. Not taking the proper time to stretch, or walk about for a brief break, can lead to back pain that might make it hard to focus on work later. Or, staring at a computer screen all day without breaks can cause a strain on your eyes that will make it harder to pay attention to what's in front of you. And not taking enough time to get proper rest or sleep can throw your entire system off, making it hard to stay alert and sharp at work the next day. But of course, I'm sure that as you're reading this, all these issues may sound like small obvious sorts of things, like the kind of things you might find in an employee manual. But that's how it gets you.

We view all these issues as small and minuscule in the grand scheme of things. We think the payoff from making these sacrifices will put our careers on the fast track or that we will be seen as "hard-workers." But that's rarely ever the case, and in an effective environment, it never is. These all snowball together and eventually plateau into a state of demotivation and worse yet, health issues.

Finding validations for negative behaviors is detrimental to your mindset and overall health.

We slowly grow to accept these discomforts as the norm. We think everyone is dealing with back problems, that we all constantly look at our screens, and if "Joe" doesn't sleep, or seems to be online late responding to emails, then I should too! Finding validations for negative behaviors like these are detrimental to your mindset and overall health. What's even worse about accepting these negative validations, is the effects of poor self-care only worsen with age. This means if we begin accepting de-energizing behaviors now, then we could be entering a long-term path of always settling for less than our best selves.

This is where the internal self-care comes into play. Sometimes, people rush into ideas of fixing their physical routines with the thought of being able to completely pull a 180. But generally, these plans end up being completely wasted due to one costly mistake. When you don't take the time to properly realign your mental state to your new-found inspiration, you will continually find yourself falling short of your goals.

Think about the dozens to hundreds of roles that make up an organization and how efficiently each role needs to perform to keep that organization afloat, let alone thrive. You can't have your quality assurance people coming in with a lack of sleep and lack of attention to detail. Your customer service workers can't be tired and fed up with dealing with customers every day due to a poor subconscious or irritable attitude.

But as smaller parts of a bigger machine, it's hard to truly feel like you can break away and take that extra time to put in some well needed R-&-R. That's why it is so important for the organization to really curate an environment that stimulates and encourages individual wellbeing. And once again, we have to return to the foundational things.

Yes, an organization may not be able to control their employees' sleep schedules but how are they influencing it? There will always be crunch times or moments where you have to pull long hours to achieve a deadline or goal, however, it shouldn't be the norm. Encouraging constant late nights, an always-on mentality, or a work-first culture, even subconsciously, is not the way to go about creating a high performance and engaged workforce. The effects of loss of sleep are costly and can damage work performance on numerous levels.

In a 2004 study, researchers at the Center of Sleep Medicine analyzed four years of data on highway car accidents involving Italian police officers. They found that napping before shifts resulted in a reduced number of collisions by 48 percent. A similar study, conducted in 2002 by Rebecca Smith-Coggins of Stanford University, analyzed a group of physicians and nurses who worked three consecutive 12-hour night shifts. The study compared a group of 26 who napped for 40 minutes at 3 AM vs a group of 23 who worked with no sleep. The group who took the extra time to rest outperformed their co-workers in a test of attention requiring them to insert a catheter in a virtual simulation. Now, of course, this doesn't mean your organization needs to a schedule a mandatory nap time for all employees. But it does show the invaluable effects of proper rest and sleep. It never hurts to take time to check on everyone's hours, suggest an early night or late morning to those who seem to be stretching themselves thin, and encourage quality rest. Being aware of how hard your workforce is pushing is key to avoiding de-energizing behaviors such as lack of self-care. No one needs a micro-manager, but a leader should never let their team continuously run themselves ragged.

While it may be easy to spot a physically worn out and drained employee, finding those in need of a quick mental check may be harder to notice. Most employees don't tend to feel comfortable mentioning they need a mental break. There is a general sense that we receive our jobs due to our mental capabilities, and if we fail to continually prove it, that there's always someone else next in line waiting for a shot at our position. This can lead to employees not wanting to admit to their moments of extra strain and forcing themselves to fight through it. One of the greatest ways to fight this is to ensure that your organization functions with a culture that reminds every individual of their value.

Taking small breaks throughout the day, to recharge and renew, can be hugely beneficial.

Making sure each employee feels heard and cared for is huge. An open and valued environment will ensure most employees feel comfortable speaking up about their current state of affairs and doing what they need to do to get that well needed break. Just make sure you're doing what you can to provide your employees with a feeling of concern and value, because fighting through those mental phases and collapses will only lead to poor work performance. A 2007 study conducted by Heleen Slagter of Leiden University measured the brain activity of 40 people in an attention test. The 40 people were split into two groups, 17 were sent to complete a three-month meditation retreat, while the other 23 were required to meditate for 20 minutes a day. Those who had made time every day to meditate outperformed those who been meditating for three months. The results of the electroencephalogram seemed to conclude that those who had been away for 90 days were less efficient due to the long break. In contrast, those who had just made a little time every day to take a mental rest were still sharp and efficient. This suggests it really doesn't require grand gestures, or considerable time investments, to support one's mental state being healthy and efficient. A small break away from the stressors of life is all it really takes to renew and continue going with an energized mindset and attitude.

Tips and Advice

From an individual perspective it is important to be mindful of your mental wellbeing and health. If you find yourself consistently spending most of your time thinking about work, or in a state of worry, it can evoke negative emotions such as anger, frustration, or hopelessness. It can stop you from being able to get the rest you need, it can impact your performance, and it can impact your relationships. Sometimes people will "handle" it through various behaviors such as drinking, eating, or shopping, but in truth they are just feeling more depressed. Some people can work towards shifting into a more energized state and take care of themselves so that they feel good, other times they may need to talk to someone who can support them in making sure their mental health and wellbeing is positive. Start with creating space for yourself, even if it is just a couple of minutes tacked onto the end of your shower. Time to connect with yourself, check in on yourself and see how you are feeling. Look at your schedule and build the time into your day. Whether it is five minutes, fifteen minutes, or an hour, just make sure you do it.

When finding it tough to practice basic self-care, such as daily movement and nutrition, we often advise people to identify the barriers. For example, if you know you find it hard to eat healthily on weekdays as you get in late from work, maybe factor in meal prep on Sunday's or have on-hand healthy snacks.

As a manager, ask yourself, are you supporting your employee's need for self-care? As when there are constantly unsustainable workloads, the first thing employees often sacrifice is their self-care. Healthy behaviors must be role modeled so that they are seen as acceptable. For example, if you as an organization have implemented unlimited vacation, but then everyone is too busy to use it, or it is not encouraged, then what is the point? It is critical that leadership role model healthy behaviors so that employees feel comfortable and understand that there are no negative repercussions for healthy activities that support them performing and feeling their best--such as taking a moment to re-energize and clear their mind throughout the day or taking a vacation.

We are seeing that more and more organizations are trying to cultivate self-care. In the past 5 years, we have seen more companies try and incorporate wellness into the workplace, often times to support efforts of saving costs on health insurance. There are all kinds of benefits to implementing workplace wellness initiatives, not just preventive care, but there are more and more studies showing that a better work/life harmony and wellness opportunities at work lead to better performance. Your programs depend on what works for your employees. How are you looking at supporting self-care? How are you providing education, tools and building awareness? How are you fostering a culture that supports physical, emotional, and mental wellbeing? There are some common methods, such as making movement fun through campaigns and competitions, access to fitness centers, onsite clinics, standing desks, healthy workspaces, and access to healthy foods, which can be considered. However, while these are helpful in removing some of the barriers to being healthy and will work to attract talent, these alone will only get an organization so far. Are you going deeper? Are you looking at areas such as stress management, emotion management or resilience, and taking a more holistic view to wellbeing?

How it can show up

If you experience a lower level of self-care...

It is likely that you need to work on increasing your basic health and wellbeing. This includes eating enough healthful foods, being active, getting adequate rest, and being kind to yourself i.e. managing your inner voice so that it works for you. An important part of self-care is not being overly critical and harsh with yourself, but being respectful and kind, especially in challenging moments. It is important to know what it feels like when your inner voice is at play in an overly judgmental and unkind way, as then you can start reworking the conversation into something that works for you in a positive way.

When you need to engage new behaviors and form healthy habits, it will help to break it down into small steps. Do not try and change everything at once. Take just one action at a time until it becomes a healthy norm. For example, eating a healthy meal every day for dinner or going to sleep at a consistent time each night.

If your team or organization experiences a lower level of self-care...

It could mean that your employees are lacking self-compassion, experiencing unsustainable workloads, and not prioritizing basic needs for nutrition, physical movement, and rest.

It could also indicate that there is a lack of a culture of wellbeing, where healthy behaviors are not supported or encouraged, and that people feel the need to sacrifice foundational wellness activities for the approval of others, progression in their careers, or the perception that they are working hard enough. This can impact employee morale, motivation, and wellbeing, and is certainly not sustainable.

CHAPTER SEVEN

Mindful Practice

Paying attention, being in the present moment, and being non-judgmental.

How often are we really ever encouraged to stop and smell the roses? It seems like common advice, yet it seems to rarely come up in workplace settings. Which is unfortunate. Ever more so, this common reminder to relax seems to lessen in occurrence as we progress through life gaining more responsibilities. One would think that this useful piece of advice would be most relevant in the always-on, overwhelming business world. So why is it that we frequently, for lack of a better phrase, forget to stop and smell the flowers?

Mindful practice doesn't necessarily stop or start with smelling the flowers. Mindful practice goes deeper. Not only asking you to smell the flowers, but consider how the flowers got there, appreciating the beauty they offer, and how the soothing scent brings you peace of mind. Nowadays, we think we can supplement mindfulness by providing an energizing ambiance to the environments of our workplaces. But games, onsite meditation, and standing desks--while helpful--aren't sufficient replacements for the various mental mindful checks and refreshers we need. Providing a healthy environment certainly sets the stage for mindfulness, but we need to go further.

Being mindful is about being in the moment and paying attention without judgement and without distraction. Whether this is in a conversation, eating mindfully, admiring the beauty of nature, or focused on a work task--it is about being absorbed in the moment. From this state, we can be more aware of our feelings and those of others. When we are absorbed in the moment, we are more engaged and can experience moments with greater intensity and clarity.

It is important to note that this is not just for eating, working, and relaxing, but also accounts for being mindful in stressful situations. Being able to listen and focus on the situation at hand by being both physically and mentally present helps positively energized people see all of the clues. Instead of occupying their minds with formulating their response to what the other person is saying, they are actively taking in what they see, feel, and hear while the other person is talking.

Being mindful is being physically and mentally present in the moment, concentrating and giving focus to the task at hand, without distraction and wandering thoughts.

Business professionals need to feel refreshed and clear so that they can focus intently on their work, not just the motion of it. This goes beyond taking long weekends, or a holiday, but comes down to those micro-moments such as stepping away to refocus your mind and replenish your energy. Think about an engine, it can only keep going so far before needing to refuel. Our minds are the same, they run better after some refueling.

So, where does mindful practice begin? It's a question that can have many answers depending on who you're asking, but there's always a starting place. The foundation for a mindful headspace starts with a clear mind. One not tainted by the pollution of busyness, multi-tasking, and negative stressors. You can try meditating or taking up a similar exercise, or maybe it is during your shower time or during a walk. However, you want to find a time where you can relax your mind and focus completely on, well, nothing at all. Just find what works best for clearing your mind. This will allow you to create a foundation for mindful stability and help with further developing a mindful attitude.

When you finally reach a point of being able to tune out, you can then begin to tune back in. The difference now being that when you tune back in, you're more finely tuned. For instance, instead of allowing yourself to shoot off a series of quick-trigger responses to fast paced or even high-stress situations, you'll now be able to digest your decisions and reactions more consciously before making them. With a clearer mind we can weave out all the extra noise and focus on the important things happening around us. We can note the potential impact of decisions we make before making them, we can understand where the issue is coming from before rushing to a solution, and, in general we can just be more in the moment--aware and prepared for what might arise. We also enable ideas to flow more freely, often seeing possibilities and solutions to challenges that couldn't enter our busy minds before. These are all healthy benefits of protecting time in our daily life for silence and reflection.

It is also important to savor moments of joy--moments where you can just be. These opportunities for escape, no matter how brief, can keep our energy stores replenished and keep us feeling and performing our best. How often do we wolf down our food (even sometimes while working at the same time) without genuinely enjoying the taste or taking the time to savor each bite? How often do we have a conversation, when really, we are thinking about something else and missing the details of what someone else is saying?

An increasing number of studies are finding positive effects of being mindful in our daily lives. A systematic review (Janssen M, Heerkens Y, Kuijer W, van der Heijden B, and Engels J, 2018) studied the effects of mindfulness-based stress reduction on employees' mental health. Based on their analysis, some of the strongest outcomes were reduced levels of emotional exhaustion, stress, depression, and anxiety. Improvements were found in terms of mindfulness, personal accomplishment, self-compassion, quality of sleep, and relaxation. It is all about seeing what works for you. How you can best become more mindful or be in the moment and then injecting it into your day.

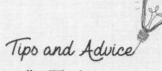

Tips and Advice

This is all about what works for you personally. Whether disconnecting, simply being in the moment, or releasing worrisome thoughts, different things work for different people. Think about the moments that absorb you. Maybe it is listening to music, watching a show, working out, taking a walk, or meditating. Whatever those moments are, it is important to create space for some of this into your day and enjoy it.

It also takes setting and maintaining boundaries that make space and protect time. For example, taking a quick stretch every 90 minutes to clear your mind before continuing with the task at hand. Or, if you know you need a few moments to decompress from work before engaging in family time, so that you can be focused and present, then perhaps structure it into your day. It could be calling someone to discuss the day and vent before you get home, it could be as simple as 10 minutes to yourself before you walk through the door. Perhaps you need to set dedicated worry time, to think about the things that are causing you concern. Setting some boundaries on allowing ourselves to feel frustration or worry for a period of time before shifting focus to family or the next activity, can help us be more present. Again, it is about finding out what works for you, so don't be afraid to experiment! It is also important to communicate your needs to those around you, such as your partner or manager. For example, letting your partner know, "I had a hard day, I'm ok, but just need 10 minutes to myself to work through it". Otherwise, relationships can be impacted. You may be physically present, but people around you will feel a disconnect as you are not emotionally or mentally present.

Programming time in our daily lives for silence and self-reflection is a key part of mindful practice. Thinking about what went well, what you would like to improve, and what actions you can take moving forward. Having time to just be with your thoughts, or in silence, helps quiet the mind, celebrate your wins, and remove the noise, which allows the fog to clear in our heads so that we can see situations with clarity. Some people find it helpful to use an app, to meditate, or to just be alone, but again, it is about figuring out what works for you.

As managers, you can be mindful of your employees' workloads. Are you supporting boundaries that respect their needs and enable them to maintain healthy boundaries so that they can spend time with their families and on their own self-care? How are you behaving? Do your employees always see you multi-tasking? Are you present in conversations with them or distracted on your phone or thinking about something else? Mindful practice means fostering teams where employees can be open about their needs. Asking your employees how they are doing, if they are managing ok, and checking in with them allows you to be active in helping support them.

Organizationally building a culture of being present takes dedicated action starting with setting the example and giving permission for others to follow. For instance, encouraging employees to take the time to eat, or perhaps looking at your meeting culture so that employees are not in back-to-back meetings all day with no time for pause. Think about it, if an employee needs to take a quick break, but in your workplace it seems like this is not the norm, or that taking a break is not the "done" thing, then they are less likely to do so.

How it can show up

If you experience a lower level of mindful practice…

It is likely that you are not as present as you need to be and that you may not be taking moments to recharge and renew. It can help to pick one activity to be mindful of. For example, eating dinner with your family without phones out, or eating lunch away from your desk, and simply starting by making sure you focus on this one activity at hand. As you become more present in this activity, you can move onto another activity. It will become easier as you build out the capability.

To start taking renewal breaks, first, you need to monitor when you start feeling restless or losing concentration. When you feel this, instead of pushing through, take a quick 10-minute break and then return to the task at hand.

If your team or organization experiences a lower level of mindful practice...

It could mean that your people are not managing their micro-moments of renewal, pushing themselves from one thing to another, and not taking those 10-minutes to re-energize. It will increase productivity if employees are encouraged to take refresher breaks, as well as increase how engaged they feel. This not only comes from having spaces for them to do so, but culturally ensuring the behavior is seen as acceptable.

It could also indicate that they are not taking moments for themselves in their daily lives--either moments to savor, moments of joy, or moments to reflect. This can lead to higher levels of stress, and less awareness, as the mind is too distracted to see things with clarity.

Another typical reason for low scores, is that there is a culture of over worrisome thoughts. This can stem from toxic workplace norms and a lack of transparent communication.

CHAPTER EIGHT

Positive Outlook

Expressing genuine gratitude and seeing the good in situations and people.

This is the expression of genuine gratitude and seeing the good in situations, even when they are challenging. If we ask ourselves, are we grateful for what we have? The likelihood is that we all say yes. However, people with higher levels of energizing behaviors practice gratitude and spend a few moments daily thinking about what they have, who they have in their lives, and what they value. Studies have shown that gratitude, especially when expressed to those you are grateful for, can lead to many benefits, including better sleep and flipping the mindset from anxious or negative states into more positive ones.

A positive attitude isn't just a feel-good spirit, nor does it mean you aren't realistic. It's a tool engineered to help you fight through any situation--no matter how difficult or sensitive it may be. This is also a powerful technique in creating an energized work spirit. Those who take on the workday, and life itself, with a positive outlook, are resilient, efficient, and are undeterred by any surprise obstacles that may arise.

People with a positive outlook see a required task as an opportunity, something they are thankfully afforded to do, rather than maybe something they "have to do." This ability helps them move past challenging moments that occur in their personal life, as well as professionally. When we can see something more positive, in even the most negative of times, we can reduce the negative impact of these moments, transforming them into an opportunity for learning, reflection, and growth.

Understanding the true meaning of wealth, beyond material possessions, also contributes to a more positive outlook. Valuing experiences and connections with others, as enablers of happiness, can help people feel like they have more in life.

Within organizations, it is important to foster an environment where people give and receive genuine, specific, worthwhile praise--for the value they bring and for who they are. This nourishes the soul and evokes a positive state of mind--simply said, it feels good. Often, you will see this practice go left. People start giving kudos for all kinds of things, without the specificity that makes it meaningful. It is important that the culture is one in which it is natural for people to be clear and specific in their acknowledgements, to bring the positive value of such behaviors.

> *Understanding the life riches that exist in experiences and relationships with others, and not just in material gains or status, contributes to positively energized people feeling and performing their best.*

Another element of a positive outlook is that it feels natural and genuine. Not a forced sense of having to be positive. Forcing a fake attitude can cause a feeling of incongruence between what people feel inside and what they demonstrate outwardly. This can add to pressure, anxiety, and stress, if they feel they have to be a certain way. It is better to acknowledge your feelings as they are, process them, and move forward. We are not always going to be happy, challenging times occur, people experience family issues and organizations experience layoffs or changes in leadership. In these moments, "acting happy" can sometimes have the opposite effect. Organizations and people can better serve themselves by acknowledging the moment, the feelings experienced, and then moving forward positively through growth and learning.

Tips and Advice

As an individual, this is about embracing all moments, even challenging or negative ones. Everything that happens to us shapes us, grows us, and helps us learn more about what we need to feel fulfilled and to be successful. We can experience tough moments throughout life, however, having a positive outlook in these situations is a choice. When you do experience a challenging moment, lean into the emotion, give yourself time and permission to feel it, and then process it. Ask yourself: What is making me feel this way? What have I learned about myself? And, what can I do next time to improve? By doing so, it is easier to learn from the situation and move forward.

Sometimes, having a positive outlook can mean reframing what success means to you. It is easy to think you will be happy when a certain milestone is achieved, such as earning a certain salary, or buying a certain car, or even a life event such as getting married. However, this can cause you to put a lot of pressure on this one thing, only to find when you get it, you still feel "off" inside. Feeling fulfilled and happy within, makes us more resilient, open to change and transition, and comfortable in times of challenge. Start by reflecting on times that you felt happy. What were you doing?

Practicing gratitude is a wonderful way to promote positive emotions. This means asking yourself frequently, what and who are you grateful for and why? Then, being in this moment and soaking up the feeling. This is a practice that you can also do as a team, or leader, to role model the behavior. If you feel you cannot work your way into a more positive space, then you may need to get some support from a coach, or a mental health professional, who can guide you and equip you with the right tools to move forward.

As a manger, it is important to help and support your employees through moments of challenge, or even organizational moments that can be dispiriting, such as a sales loss. Often, you will be in a position where you're required to answer for the decisions made above you. For example, organizational cutbacks, layoffs, strategic changes, or organizational change. It is all about looking at what you can do to cultivate a positive organizational culture, that is within your control, as how these situations are handled will impact your employees' emotional stability. This can help prevent the rumor mill from spiraling and prevents negative emotions from festering. It can help to take away feelings of anger that can come from employees feeling that they are not in the loop as well as let them know they are valued, appreciated, and that you are available for them.

Another way is to facilitate meaningful praise, as this makes employees feel higher levels of positivity. Sometimes, when a manager finds this tough, we find it stems back to experiences they had as an employee, or the role of praise in their life. There are all kinds of ways to acknowledge people, and how you do will depend on the person and how you can let them know in the best way for them. Think about how they contributed to the outcome and why it is meaningful to them. For example, did they do something challenging? Or, did they, go above and beyond? Also, be sure to look for smaller victories along the way, not just the obvious big outcomes. For example, if you land a big client, think about all the things people have done along the way to make that happen. This may include the person that made the presentation, or the person that welcomed in the client to the meeting, as all of these people played a role in the success.

Organizationally, transparent, open communications promote positive feelings. In difficult times especially, employees need to feel supported through the transition and change. Don't keep them in limbo and don't be cryptic with your messages, as this all keeps them in a state of worry. Instead, ensure communications are clear, timely, and provide employees a path to ask questions.

How it can show up

If you experience a lower level of positive outlook...

It is likely that you are not experiencing enough positive moments such as receiving meaningful, specific praise (which could be from your manager, coworker, partner, friends or family), or frequently practicing gratitude. Every day, it can help to start thinking about what you are grateful for and why, as well as what you feel good about that day and why. The positivity from this can be elevated by telling people what you appreciate about them and why, or by sharing good news.

You may also find it challenging to see the good in difficult or challenging moments. To start cultivating this mindset, it can help to identify what about you or your life, is better after you have been through a situation. For example, what knowledge do you now have that you didn't before? Even if it is the knowledge that you can get through tough times, it is something positive that makes you stronger.

If your team or organization experiences a lower level of positive outlook...

It could mean that your employees are not exposed to enough positive interactions. These can include receiving and giving meaningful, specific praise, having conversations that promote positivity, or having enough enriching experiences with others.

It could also indicate that there is a lack of cultivating an environment of growth and learning, where individuals can lean on each other to learn and expand their perspectives in challenging times. This includes a lack of sharing and having honest discussions regarding lessons learned and feelings.

This can impact their overall positive wellbeing as the more exposure we have to draining negativity, the more it can negatively impact how we feel. It is important to lean into challenging times and acknowledge negative emotions, which serve as important indicators, to learn and move forward from.

CHAPTER NINE

Purpose & Meaning

Being connected to a greater purpose and having a focus on what brings oneself satisfaction.

This is about looking beyond yourself. This does not have to be a massive or grand thing. It means something that you are living for, beyond your immediate circumstances, which enables you to see the true value in what you are doing.

This could be anything from understanding how your role at work betters the lives of your consumers, how your duty aids in keeping your entire organization running efficiently, or understanding how the work you do helps you provide for your family or even yourself. Whatever the reason, understanding how you spend your time aligns best to what you find meaningful, is something you can draw energy from every day.

In fact, research has shown that having a sense of purpose in life appears to widely buffer against mortality risk across the adult years, and, may even help combat stress.

There are a couple of ways that people can feel a sense of meaning. First, understanding the purpose and meaning around the business that they are a part of that truly resonates with them. Then, looking at what they really need to feel successful in the workplace, what makes them feel good, and what is important to them. People have to determine what they need to feel valued. Once they become aware of this, it is easier to correlate it to positions, to connect to roles, their responsibilities, and the organization itself.

We spend so much of our time working and interacting with people. It is imperative to understand what is truly important to you so that you can think about your time and efforts. Will spending time on something be fulfilling for you?

The best place to feel fulfilled is when you experience purpose and meaning. When we feel good about what we do, and we see the value of what we do, we thrive. It causes us to face challenges in a more positive way and we connect better with others. In our personal life, it is all about what works and what doesn't. Even looking at the purpose and meaning within relationships can go a long way. Professionally, it is looking at career choices and learning about what you like and don't like, when you are at your best and when you are not. Looking back at roles and thinking about what felt good to you, and what didn't, can help you identify the patterns and characteristics of what is best for you. You can then work to make the necessary shifts and reposition as needed.

Taking the organizational lens, this starts with your mission. What are your organizational goals and what does this mean for your customers and employees? So often, we focus so intently on the customers and profits that we can forget the need for a fulfilled and positive workforce. After all, why you exist as an organization is the very reason that all these people dedicate so many hours of their week to various tasks and activities.

Imagine Tina, she works for a financial services company. She really loves the fact that they are helping people realize their dreams. The company does customer roadshows where she gets to meet some of the people they have helped. She fondly recalls a husband and wife who had experienced a challenging time, having a newborn and then the husband being laid off. Through one of the company's programs, the couple managed to turn an idea of a daycare into a business. While Tina loves helping people, she realized that over time, leadership and investors seemed to be caring less and less. It was becoming more about the bottom line, at the expense of the humans that they were helping. She sees more and more decisions being made that are not always the best for the people they are serving. What happens? Well, eventually she feels misaligned. The very value and purpose she held, that drove her and motivated her to work harder and achieve more for the business, is now not there. Eventually, this leads to demotivation and often attrition. This is not to say that profit is not important, but rather, that the values and purpose should be the compass for the behaviors demonstrated.

The purpose should be threaded through in everything, built right into the language, retention plans, development, diversity, on-boarding, succession planning, and upward mobility. If it is treated like an afterthought to any of this then your organization has failed. For companies where the purpose is threaded through, even when tremendous changes happen (which they always do), these companies are able to continue, try new things, and persevere.

Managers play a significant role in helping make sure that employees are connected and can correlate their role and efforts to an aligned purpose. By identifying their employees' strengths, and understanding what keeps them happy and fulfilled, managers can better find the right opportunities for their employees. Taking the time to understand what motivates each individual, their personal and professional goals, and drawing a clear line of sight to how they contribute to the purpose of the company, supports an engaged and productive team.

Tips and Advice

As an individual you can focus a bit more on self-exploration. What in your life is providing you a sense of meaning? It may be time spent outside of work, on projects, or in service of others. It could be that you feel the contributions you make at work are a part of something meaningful. When you look at work, ask yourself if the larger mission of your organization, and purpose, resonates with you. Is it something you are passionate about? This all helps you discover your personal why. Why do you do what you do? It is important to not only be upfront about this with yourself, but with your organization as well. This can start as early as the interview process, asking about company values, and continue throughout your career path. It is important you know how the company is instilling those values and what steps the company is actively taking to live out those values.

If you find yourself always busy, yet feeling like something is missing or feeling unfulfilled, then it is worth spending some time thinking about what is meaningful to you and what you need to feel valued, successful, and fulfilled. Look at the times you have felt really good in your life, and the times that you haven't felt good. Make a list so that you can see the patterns, as then you can work to infuse more of what makes you feel good and fulfills you into your daily life. The more you spend time and energy on the things that make you happy, the higher levels of self-worth you have and the more collaborative and creative you are.

Managers must ask themselves are we valuing our employees? Celebrating them? Growing them? As a manager, it is important to help employees see a clear line between what they do and how they spend their time, to the mission, larger goal, and organizational why. Acknowledge what it is about their work and who they are that brings value and let them know how they contributed to achieving goals as well as how they contribute to the team. When we understand our place and contributions, we feel a sense of belonging. Sometimes an organization is "doing good", but employees do not feel a part of it, or as if what they do isn't really contributing as much as other people. In these cases, it is important to be clear on their values and strengths as individuals and collectively in the team. It is also important to understand their areas for enhancement, as this can help you align them to opportunities for growth that can elevate a sense of meaning.

Organizationally, it is paramount to understand your 'Why'. Why does your organization exist? You could be achieving meaningful impact among a wide consumer base or even globally, but all of that is undercut within your company if such achievement is not communicated among your workforce. Sharing stories, such as stories from customers, or about the social good the organization is doing, can help your employees feel a part of it. Every employee plays a role, so it is about looking at how your employees play a role in bringing your purpose to life.

How it can show up

If you experience a lower level of purpose and meaning....

It is likely that you are not spending time and energy on things that are providing you with a feeling of purpose, that you are not seeing or feeling the valuable contributions you are making, or that you are feeling as though you can do more. A first step is identifying what makes you feel fulfilled. What types of activities make you feel like you are providing value? Then you can work to bring more of these into your life. It can help to look at ways in which you help others, whether it is being there for a friend or volunteering, as this can provide a sense of purpose and meaning.

If your team or organization experiences a lower level of purpose and meaning...

It could mean that your employees are not feeling valued. They may not understand how they contribute to the bigger picture, they may feel far removed from the customers or business goals, or they may not feel that they are using their strengths enough.

It could also indicate that employees are not able to contribute value in a way that energizes them or that they feel their work is not recognized or important. This can lead to them feeling like they are a cog in a machine, or just a "body" to the company, which can cause lower levels of motivation and engagement.

CHAPTER TEN

Relationships

Fostering high quality, healthy, and authentic connections with others.

It is said that human connection and interaction is a powerful driver of our human nature. Connecting and learning with others is what reminds us of compassion and empathy, two things needed to empower our inner and social growth. The relationships we create, and the bonds we carry with us, leave a big impression on us and even provide some insight into the type of person we are or who we aspire to be. No matter the case, one thing is certain, when we neglect to dedicate time to nurturing meaningful relationships, we are not only neglecting a piece of ourselves but missing out on a key energizer.

It can be easy to forget that sometimes relationships need a proactive dedication to foster their growth. Sure, there is going to be that set of people in your life who will always be there for you no matter how far apart you are. However, this is not a justification for missing opportunities to purposefully connect and show care. Healthy, positive relationships require a consistent amount of dedication. This doesn't mean going out of the way to plan a big trip with your family every weekend. And it doesn't have to mean going out of your way to show some grand display of appreciation either. But it does mean putting in a bit of effort to check in with someone and acknowledging that there is a genuine relationship there. A call once a week, messaging a funny picture you know they'll enjoy, or maybe you can invite them to get a quick cup of coffee with you. Relationships aren't stagnant things, they are always growing as the people involved are growing themselves, and if the people continue growing forward while the relationship stays the same then eventually you can grow apart. If you wait until a relationship that you care about feels as if it is fading away before you work on it, then you've waited too long...but it's never too late to start.

It's not easy. A part of growing is getting busy with the everyday responsibilities of life and it doesn't get any easier when everyone around you begins to get busy too. People get caught up in the stress and exhaustion of their careers, feel drained after work hours, and can tend to prefer an early night's rest over a phone call with a loved one. But a choice in one moment can quickly turn into a whole month of no communication, and suddenly it's not just an occasional decision, it's a frequent habit. If people feel you are too busy for them then they themselves may even decide to stop putting so much effort into nurturing your bonds. It is not to say that you need to always be connecting with others or consistently putting the needs of others above your own. We all need alone time and time to rest. It is to say, that proactively spending time with the people that matter to you is critical to your wellbeing, so you need to create space for this, in a way that is manageable for you.

It goes beyond just being available for people when they need you, but being proactive, and making space in your life, to connect with those that matter to you.

Many feel that it is ok to just be there when people need you. Indeed, it is a great trait that people think you are dependable in their times of need. However, thinking this way can limit the amount of proactive effort you put into cultivating your relationships. Having meaningful relationships as a frequent part of your life includes those connections with friends, family, and colleagues. Meaningful relationships are a great way to not only recharge purpose and satisfaction in your life but catalyze growth, inspiration, and excitement. This is especially powerful when you find yourself beginning to get lost in the repetitive stress of work, personal responsibility, and general upkeep. We grow close to certain kinds of people for a reason. Whether it is because they understand us, they bring us joy, or they simply inspire us to do more, there's a reason. Really dig deep and try to understand what that reason may be for you. Maybe a relationship feels it is fading away because you don't still feel that original connection that brought you together, and that's ok. All that means is that maybe your energy is best placed elsewhere. But if that reason still holds true in even the slightest, then that relationship is worth valuing, as that person provides your life with an important energizer.

When we set aside time each day to focus on our relationships with others, we can feel happier. Not spending enough time with friends and family has been found to be one of the greatest regrets people have in life. In fact, a longitudinal study from researchers at Harvard, one of the world's longest studies of adult life, demonstrated that our relationships and how happy we are in our relationships have a powerful influence on our health.

Given that we spend so much of our time working and collaborating, nurturing relationships plays a large role at work. Making sure people feel valued and appreciated, making sure employees can spend the time to get to know each other as people, and forming connections with others at work, can help employees feel more motivated and enable them to be more collaborative. When we feel we know others for who they are as people, and connect on that deeper level, a bond of trust is formed which supports the free flow of ideas--a must for any innovative organization.

Tips and Advice

Individually, it is important to take time to assess our relationships and make sure they are healthy and supportive. This includes having people in all areas of your life that you feel good around, that encourage you, that lift you up, and that listen to you. In life, you can start by thinking about your relationships and ask yourself:

- Do I feel good around that person?
- Can I be open and share my ideas and thoughts without fear of judgement?
- Does that person bring out my best qualities?
- Is the relationship reciprocal?

There are clear cut signs to look out for. For example, if you find yourself surrounded with people that drain you, in relationships where you are not valued or celebrated, or with people who consistently take more than they give. If you find your relationships are "off", then you need to redirect, re-shift or, sometimes, stop investing energy into certain relationships; professional and personal. After all, people will reveal themselves to you over time, you have to be open to the clues, and then it is up to you to act on that information in a way that protects your time, energy, and relationship investments. It takes work to build healthy, high quality relationships. We can find ourselves knowing many people, yet still feeling alone. It is important to create some space to build high quality connections. Start with a small objective, maybe taking 10 minutes each week to reach out to someone in your life or to see how they are doing.

While you do not need to have "best friends" at work, there is much evidence showing that having people at work that you can talk to, bounce ideas with, and vent with is good for wellbeing. If you find yourself feeling alone, or lacking a sense of belonging, you can start by setting up some time to get to know your colleagues better. Perhaps try getting a quick coffee or taking a walk and talking. Perhaps there are employee resource groups you can join. By finding ways to connect and get to know people, you will naturally form bonds from which you can spend time growing and nurturing the relationship.

Managers also need to be supported as individuals. It is important that they feel heard, valued and respected. It is also important that they foster healthy, supportive, respectful relationships with their employees. This means knowing who employees are as people.

Knowing their goals, their needs and their workstyles can help managers best support, value, communicate, and grow their employees. Start by having conversations with employees to gain insight. You can check if you are being a supportive leader by asking yourself, are you:

- Providing feedback and guidance on how to be successful at the company?
- Advocating for your employees?
- Building trust with your employees?
- Providing your employees with career growth opportunities such as different projects, travel, promotion, or helping them find opportunities?
- Paying attention in communications?

Communication plays a significant role in creating quality connections and relationships. It is especially important to be approachable and be present in communications. This means actively listening to your employees and being present without wandering thoughts or being busy preparing a response. When you actively listen, you are listening on many levels. Hearing their words, seeing their body language, and feeling their energy can all provide vital clues. Being in tune with what people are saying helps drive deeper, higher quality connections. As a leader this is critical to best serving your employees and enabling you to ask better questions.

For leaders and managers, you control the flow of team dynamics and energy. It is important to understand when there is someone exhibiting negative behaviors that may need to be addressed before it causes more stress or negative emotions for others. Do not be afraid to document what is not working and to strengthen your organization by letting truly toxic people go.

Ask yourself, as a workplace, are we creating the space for connections to be made? It is important to create an environment where employees can get to know each other, as this is what creates a community feel.

How it can show up —————————

If you experience a lower level in relationships...

It is likely that you are not spending enough time fostering high quality, reciprocal relationships. It can help to think about each of your relationships in turn and see if you are spending time nurturing them as well as if they are healthy. Maybe you need to make more effort to talk to someone, maybe someone really isn't a meaningful relationship for you anymore...whatever you find, it is important to take action to create, maintain, and grow healthy, quality relationships in your life.

If your team or organization experiences a lower level in relationships...

It could mean that people are not spending time forming, maintaining, and growing relationships beyond their roles and responsibilities for work. When you look deeper there could be several reasons. A common cause is that they feel there is no time to do so or that the organization does not invest in initiatives that expose them to opportunities to get to know their colleagues as people.

It could also indicate that they do not feel comfortable spending time connecting on topics other than work. Sometimes this can be a cultural outcome. If the workplace culture does not encourage relationship building behaviors, then employees can steer away from it.

This can impact whether employees feel open to being themselves and whether they will contribute their ideas and opinions, which can decrease the level of innovation and engagement.

CHAPTER ELEVEN

Solution Focus

Having the ability to move past frustrating situations and challenging circumstances with a view to growth, learning, and problem-solving.

Y ou could say there are two kinds of mindsets in the world. The mindset of the energized is the solution focused mindset, ready to keep growing and moving forward. The other is the mindset of someone stuck on their de-energizing habits or lost in challenging moments. The latter mindset can come face to face with a mental blocker and not be able to see any way around it. They stare at that obstacle as if a door has just been locked in their face and the key was thrown away. That person doesn't even consider looking or turning away from that locked door and finding another route. They can only imagine what the other side might have looked like had that door opened.

On the flip side, the "doer" mindset doesn't believe in locks. They face blockers head-on, with a ready-to-try-the-next-plan attitude. If a door shuts in their face, they try seeing if they can crawl through a window. All it comes down to is one person's ability to be focused on the next possibility and the other's lack of ability to adapt or move forward. If we allow ourselves to believe there is only one solution to solving a problem, then we have failed before we've tried to succeed. There are always many paths to the desired outcome. Sometimes, we may not like the journey, but most often we find that the pit stops, or detours, are a necessary part of our goal's path.

A solution focused attitude is the high-powered compass of success. We're all aware that no one has ever reached the pinnacle of their goals without stumbling once or twice along the road. A solution focused individual tends to jump into any situation understanding they may not get it right the first time. They also understand that there will be challenges, obstacles, and moments in which they are disappointed or frustrated. Think of the last time you planned something that went perfectly according to plan? If we are honest, it doesn't tend to happen often. What you'll find is that those who focus too much on the failure of the plan, and not the next step to move forward, rarely even get close to their goals, desired outcomes, or dreams.

When challenging moments occur, acknowledge your feelings and explore why you feel that way. Process the moment and progress forward with the learnings, and growth, that the situation has brought you. Often, we are in a place of greater knowledge, greater strength, and elevated capabilities after we have worked through challenges, hindrances, or adversity.

Now, this is not to say that you ignore looking at why something failed, or why you feel a certain way, it is to say that you don't get stuck there. The goal is to not get lost in rumination and to limit over worrisome thoughts. You want to process and progress, rather than replay the situation over and over again for weeks to come. If you often struggle with moving past a failure or tough moment, then that doesn't necessarily mean that you don't have the ability to focus on the next solution or move on. It's not about having some special "X-factor" or hidden gene in your DNA. All you need to do is recognize the blockers that continue to plague you with this de-energizing mindset.

How you deal with your emotions in a state of failing, or in a challenging situation, plays a crucial role in how well you will move forward. The most de-energizing behavior you can continue is giving too much energy to your negative emotions. Allowing yourself to wallow in guilt, embarrassment, or anger is the equivalent of cannonballing into a pit of quicksand. By no means is it easy to get over personal attachments but there are ways to avoid this. First, consider your reaction. It's tempting to jump into instant frustration when things don't work out the way we wanted. If you're one of those people who can't control their initial reactions too well then maybe do some prep work. Prepare ahead of time for what might go wrong, already start finding ways to understand why it's nothing to fret over and already consider some next moves. Even just having a slither of positivity in the face of that initial let down might be enough to get your head back in the game.

Another behavior to watch out for is how hard you over analyze the issue. Taking an analytical look at a failing is a good thing--when done right. If you're simply using your analysis to continue to fault yourself and force further guilt upon yourself then you're not helping the situation at all. What is helpful is to simply understand why things might not have worked out the way you hoped and using the knowledge to better prepare the next strategy. The important part is that you know there may be a million reasons why things didn't fall into place as you hoped, and some of those reasons may not have been within your control.

Maybe you felt that you had been turning in some great work lately at the office, but that fancy promotion was passed over to someone you felt hadn't worked as hard.

The worst thing you can do is let that moment deflate your motivation and ruin all that hard work you have been putting in. Instead, pause, and try to take in all the factors. Maybe the newly promoted coworker wasn't working as hard as you in one aspect but was shining in another aspect, which may have been more pertinent to the role, something you maybe didn't even see. Learn from that and try to add that on to your already astounding skill set. Or, take an even more proactive approach and try communicating with leadership about why you may have been passed up or pitch your case for the next available promotion early on to make sure they're really paying attention to your performance. As long as you continue looking for moments to grow from your shortcomings, or challenges, and apply those learnings to a better and improved strategy, then you'll find a way to overcome your roadblocks.

The key is making sure you move forward in a positive cycle of growth. By being able to acknowledge your emotions (both positive and negative), objectively look at a situation, take pause, and move beyond initial reactions, you will see things with greater clarity. This can help reduce your levels of stress and ensures that temporary negative emotions do not linger on into more permanence than they should.

Having a growth mindset, rather than a fixed one, has been found to have many benefits as people with a growth mindset see their traits as changeable and, therefore, they are more resilient in difficult moments. According to research by Dr. Mary Murphy, Associate Professor of Psychology at Indiana University, organizations can exhibit either a fixed or growth mindset, same as do students. A focus on growth places importance on learning new skills and making valuable contributions, rather than just praise and recognition alone. These organizations give praise wisely, being specific and meaningful. They have a focus on their employees' journey of growth and potential. They also focus on cultivating resilience. Providing employees with techniques and strategies to help them navigate change can help them deal with not just the everyday stressors, but organizational uncertainties and bigger challenging moments.

Tips and Advice

We all make mistakes. Throughout life we will find ourselves in a plethora of uncomfortable situations, where we can experience emotions such as guilt, shame, disappointment, frustration, or anger. While focused time for reflection on these moments can be good for growth and moving forward, it does not come without its cautions. You cannot allow yourself to dwell. Putting these disappointing outcomes on an endless replay loop will only serve as torture, force your mind to relive the antagonizing emotions evoked and create new barriers that keep you from your truly authentic self. Not to mention, this cycle of rumination can result in unnecessary sleepless nights, higher levels of stress, and destructive behaviors potentially impacting your relationships and work, or having other negative consequences.

When you feel emotions rising, have a dialogue with yourself. Ask yourself, what made me feel this way? Why did this happen? If someone else is involved and the situation allows it, reach out and try to get feedback that helps you make sense of the situation. When you encounter a tough moment, give yourself permission to take a pause to feel the emotion. We find that many people try to combat these moments by trying to ignore how they feel or telling themselves they are stupid to keep thinking about it. This rarely works, as it is still there somewhere and may manifest itself in another way. Our emotions serve as important indicators that we need to take a moment, reflect, recognize, and think about what we can do moving forward. Processing your feelings is key. It is about finding what works for you. Perhaps write about it, talk about it, or just spend time creating your go-forward plan. Whatever you need to move on productively and positively.

Life is one big journey of learning. Each experience, positive or negative, provides us with valuable insights from which we can grow, improve, and forge a better future. It is therefore important, that in these challenging moments, you make sure you forgive yourself. This freeing practice moves you into a productive headspace. It is also important if you find you cannot get out of a negative space, or find yourself stuck in negative emotions where you feel you cannot move forward, that you take constructive action to move into a more positive space. This can mean asking for help, seeking professional support, or sometimes creating distance between you and the cause of the negative responses.

For managers, it is important to be ok with change and realize that you do not control everything. It is about looking at how you are encouraging employees to process moments and move forward. For example, when something happens, do you address it and talk about it in productive ways? Or, do you try to validate a decision, sweep over it, and hope they do not want to discuss it? Having the conversation, talking about what you have learned from these moments as a team, and discussing what actions to take, raises the level of comfort and creates an open forum for progress. Sometimes, you will come to a decision and then things will change. Leadership may change strategic direction or the allocation of funds. That's ok. You can learn, adapt, and amend. Continuous improvement is the real solution, for you, your team, and your projects. Constantly taking in new information that comes to light, thinking about what this means to you, your team, and projects, and then adapting in the best way to meet the goals.

Energy is contagious, so it is important to be mindful of your language and how you use your words. For example, if you tend to amplify situations. This is when a situation may be bad, or frustrating, but the language you use makes it feel like the most frustrating or worst thing in the world. Permit yourself a moment to digest information so that negative energy is not passed through to your employees and you can have a more productive conversation.

Organizationally, ask yourself, how are you cultivating resilience? As an employee, as leaders, as co-workers, we can feel hurt, anger, resentment, and disappointment. Do you practice development and foster cultural behaviors that support building resiliency muscles? The other part, is creating comfortable and welcoming environments so that all people feel safe to address their feelings, seek the information they need to resolve them, and feel supported. No matter the severity of a situation, it is important that employees feel supported by their peers. That they do not feel at risk to process, feel they can ask questions, and have the necessary discussions.

How it can show up

If you experience a lower level of solution focus...

It is likely that you struggle with moving past challenging moments, tend to feel guilty, or tend to dwell and ruminate. It may help when you experience negative situations to spend a moment to think about how you feel and acknowledge those feelings. Then, you can think about what you could have done differently and what you can learn from the experience. From this space, you can decide how you will change your actions in the future as well as best understand if there is anything you can do to remedy the situation or make necessary apologies.

If your team or organization experiences a lower level of solution focus...

It could mean that employees are holding on to negative emotions or feel too uncomfortable to discuss situations that are challenging. It can be a sign of an environment that is not open, in which employees do not feel safe and secure to discuss their thoughts or feelings. Without processing moments that are challenging, negative emotions can linger and impact the individual, as well as those around them.

It could also indicate that there are some elements of a toxic culture where there are many negative emotions or a focus on everything that can go wrong, rather than a culture of encouragement and support.

It can help to role model solution focused behaviors by discussing challenging moments openly when they occur and conducting collective sessions such as lessons learned.

CHAPTER TWELVE

Support Network

Utilizing a strong support system.

It can be hard to admit when we've hit an obstacle that we can't overcome. Most of the time it's hard to even tell when we've come to a challenge that we can't surpass ourselves. It can be different for everyone. Whether it be an ego that refuses to acknowledge weakness, an arrogance that refuses to be told what to do, or a fear that stresses over external perceptions, we all have our reasoning for thinking we can take on the world alone. While it is positive to have a do-it-yourself attitude, not knowing when it's time to lean on others can be detrimental to an energized mindset.

Without a proper network of support, it can be hard to keep moving forward. We've all been knocked down once or twice by hard times and tough situations. And while it is never impossible to get back up on your own, it can still be quite a challenge. The truth is, not having an established web of support means that the knocks hit us that much harder and getting back up takes that much longer. A great flow of support can double as a shield and safety net, there to catch us when we trip too close to the edge, there to calm us down, there to listen when we need to let something out, and there to make sure we know it is going to be ok. It's about not only understanding that sometimes we won't be able to handle everything that comes our way on our own, but being ok with this idea.

When we face challenges, big or small, we can lose a lot of the motivation and drive that comes with an energized mindset. And sure, it's possible to reclaim that energy, but that doesn't mean it'll be easy. We lose a lot when we come across failure or disappointment, and it can take a lot to gain back what we lost. That's why it is so vital to keep a solid group of support around you because, without it, we can easily become lost in a state of disappointment or hopelessness.

How you establish your support system can be just as important to your success as well. Your support network is there to remind you of the fulfilling and purposeful reasons you even attempted something to begin with. Sure, you may not have succeeded at achieving your dream job as soon as you wanted, but that doesn't mean you should lose sight of what it was. They also know how to tell you to slow down when you might be getting too ahead of yourself. Their honest and outside perspectives will help to keep you on track. For example, if you want to run a 5k, but you haven't even been on a treadmill in months, there are various types of support you will need. Make sure you have people in your support group who will openly remind you that you may need to work up to the marathon for your own health and wellbeing, offer to train with you to motivate you, or come and cheer for you in your big moment. According to a 2010 study published in Psychological Science, people with the highest levels of wellbeing engaged in deeper, more substantive conversations with their friends. To engage in these types of conversations, you need to have trust, respect, and feel your perspective is valued.

Your support group can even motivate you to keep going when you're close to that goal but begin to give up along the challenging journey. The most important thing about your support network is that they know who you are, which means knowing when to tell you to keep going, slow down, stop, or that you're doing fine just as you are. A study published in the Journal of Experimental Social Psychology showed that when we feel we have social support, our perception of challenges changes--they appear smaller and easier to deal with.

It is worth remembering, support networks are not just a positive for you, they have a positive impact on those that help and support you. In fact, according to a study by the National Institute of Health, when you help others you give off positive energy, which is contagious to those around you.

Supportive relationships include people that you can be yourself with, who you respect, who share your values, and who you feel positively around. When you cultivate these types of supportive relationships and spend time being a supportive party to them, you will find yourself feeling happier.

Tips and Advice

We all need support and how you create your support team will depend on your needs across your professional and personal life. In your personal life, it could be people you admire and trust, that you are comfortable discussing life's challenges or your fears with, and who can offer you advice from their experience. Or, if you are not fulfilled by work, they could provide support that is more around your passion or side projects that energize you. For example, if you are an analyst but enjoy art, your support network may include people from your profession as well as creatives, as they may be able to guide more creativity into your life. In your professional life, it is important to have both mentors and sponsors. Mentors can give you advice, encourage you, and support you. A sponsor is that person that will make things happen for you. Often, they are more senior and have more political equity. They will put you forward for opportunities and be an action-led advocate for you. This kind of sponsorship is earned. It comes from seeing your value. Your support network may change throughout the various phases in your life and as your needs change, so it is worthwhile periodically checking in with yourself, what your goals are, and how you are progressing, so that you can best identify your needs and the type of support that will best help.

If you need to start growing your support network, just start thinking about the people in your life. Who would you go to for different advice? Life advice? Or, to discuss a big decision moment such as a career change or opportunity? It doesn't have to be a formal thing, but personally identifying who you would go to, and then spending time building that relationship, will all positively improve your career trajectory. When you are looking to meet new people for your support network, it can be helpful to understand how to talk about yourself. For example, who you are, what you do, and what you are looking for or your goals--in this way you can start to build a network.

As a manager, ask yourself, how do you play a role in your employees' support network? This can depend on your ability to mentor and coach. However, if you do not have the capacity for this, even being able to connect employees with people, or suggesting people for them to connect with and making introductions, helps support them. Do you foster an environment where employees feel it is safe to be vulnerable and ask for help? For example, if someone doesn't know how to do something, but they fear telling you, this not only causes them stress and concern, but is not productive and impacts team performance. Having a clear view of your employees' personality, strengths, and areas for enhancement, can help you pair them up for projects in which the experience can be a supportive and learning one.

It would be amiss to not mention that it is also important that managers build a healthy support network for themselves. Often, managing people can be filled with moments that you need to discuss or get advice on. It is important that you have trusted people you can do this with, outside of your team.

Organizationally, it is about building an environment for people to connect and form supportive bonds. When it comes to mentors, many organizations have a mentor program. However, it is clear that many "mentorship programs" are flawed, often forcing connections based on points such as area of expertise or role. These can fail as the mentor-mentee relationship needs to be organic, where the mentor has a real interest in the mentee and there is a natural and authentic connection between them. Then, it is a reciprocal relationship where both mentor and mentee are gaining value. When this occurs, mentors are invaluable for employees for bouncing ideas, giving truthful feedback, and inspiring them, and mentees are invaluable to their mentors, providing fresh perspective, energizing interactions, and an opportunity to give back in meaningful ways.

How it can show up

If you experience a lower level in support network...

It is likely that you are lacking a support network or do not feel you can go to the one you have. It is important to think about why the people in your life are not providing the support you need. What are they doing, or not doing, that is making you feel as though they are not being as supportive as you need? What could you be doing better to ensure they know what you need? Sometimes, people are not supporting us in the way we need as we never took the time to communicate our needs to them.

It can also help to think about the characteristics that you need from a support network. Once you determine the traits and behaviors you need, you can then start forming the right relationships.

If your team or organization experiences a lower level in support network...

It could mean that people are not feeling supported or encouraged by those around them. They may feel they that are not truly heard, that their value is not seen, or that they are not valued.

It could also indicate that the behavior of asking for help is not encouraged. People may fear how they will be perceived if they do or think that it may hinder their professional progression.

This can impact morale and engagement as well as hinder innovation and productivity. When people feel they do not have supportive relationships, they are less open about ideas and sharing their perspectives. When they fear asking for help, they may continue working in a less than efficient way, when someone else could have collaborated and arrived at a better outcome much faster.

"Wellbeing is not a soft benefit – it's a necessity.
It's not just an HR discussion, it's a profit
discussion. And companies that understand this and
embrace the new science will win the future."

Arianna Huffington

FINAL WORDS

There you have it. The 12 factors that will enable you, your teams, and organizations to perform and feel their best! I hope that some of what you have read has made you think about ways in which you can engage in behaviors that enable a healthier and happier you, as well as enrich the lives of those around you.

I hope that it also got you thinking about the various elements that lead to programs that build the underlying behaviors and mental muscles that lead to energized, productive, engaged, and resilient people. I'll leave you with two things. Firstly, a couple of real-life examples that demonstrate some of the challenges we have seen and how the practical application of carefully crafted development programs, combined with data and insights, can help expedite the journey to positive, sustained change. Secondly, some questions to get you thinking about where your organization is currently, next steps, and where to start first!

Some examples...

 Jim, the Sales Executive ————————————————

 Jim is a sales executive working for a large corporation who travels at least once a month. He has not felt good about himself for a while, slowly gaining weight from all of the client meals out and the life of travel is taking a toll. Three months ago, he started working out, and although he is doing everything right, he still isn't feeling great. He keeps trying different plans, different foods, and he hopes that at some point it will work. However, he is getting more and more demotivated as he is not seeing the results. His energy is shifting, and his confidence is decreasing, which is not great for a role that requires a high positive energy when dealing with clients.

After taking an evaluation that looks at Jim's behavioral norms, it is identified that:

- He uses his professional lifestyle of travel as a justification for behaviors such as eating, drinking, and not fitting in his exercise while travelling.
- He is stressed, from the guilt and pressure of leaving his family for business travel.
- The meetings themselves are causing him stress due to the fact that he is carrying some of the work others should have been doing. He has not addressed this, and these emotions have been bottled up inside.

With this knowledge, he moves into a coached development program in which his negative belief systems are broken down and he is taught the mental processes and coping strategies he needs. This elevates the value of his fitness regime and accelerates the achievement of his goals. By learning the triggers of his stress, and coping strategies to reduce it, he is able to achieve his fitness goals without the impact of stress hindering his progress.

 Lucy, the Manager ——————————————————

Lucy is a manager on her company's leadership track. Lucy goes to an empowerment event for women that her company has put on to help develop their female leadership. It is AMAZING. Amazing speakers, inspirational panels, and thought-provoking workshops. She is buzzed. Her mind is racing with all of the things she is going to do to achieve what she wants. As the days pass, the norms of work and personal life unfold. Months later she looks back and realizes she didn't get to do any of the things she wanted to do--life had gotten in the way once again. The company realizes that they are not getting their desired returns on the event, so the next time her company has an event, they design it with development in mind. Before the event, all the attendees are given an evaluation so that they can become aware of their areas of opportunity. Lucy gets her overview and realizes she needs help:

- Living her values to reduce cognitive dissonance.
- Being able to communicate the reasons behinds her opinions and perspective.

During the event, they kick off with a look at the collective data patterns which desensitizes everyone, allowing Lucy to feel safe that she is not alone in her struggles. She then attends the workshops correlated to her needs, and afterwards, she has a take-away workbook that is tailored to her exact behavioral blockers. Now, she can continue the momentum by working on engaging small new behaviors that grow into natural habits. This, combined with a mobile app to help track her progress, allows her to apply her learnings in the context of her real life.

 ### *Rob, the SVP*

Rob is an SVP at a large banking company. A while ago he realized he was too stressed and tired from the emotional roller coaster of being a leader as there are so many responsibilities and always fires to put out. He has been using a meditation app for a while, and overall, it is helping him be generally calmer and more relaxed. However, today, he has a bad meeting and his manager and stakeholders are not happy. He is under pressure. He wishes he could use his app quickly, but he has to go to another meeting, so off he goes, stressed and filled with negative emotions. Rob realizes he needs to work on reacting better to situations in the moment. He takes an evaluation to better understand his behaviors, mental processes, and feelings. He finds that he:

- Cannot process negative situations well.
- There is a correlation to his tendency to personalize everything.

With this knowledge, he continues doing weekly exercises which build the mental processes needed to internalize and respond to challenging situations. Now, he can draw on the calmness he experiences from the meditation app which, over time, helps him decrease his general stress levels. He can also apply a stronger mental process in the moment, during challenging situations, without letting them negatively impact his day.

What is the key from these real-life examples? That all transformation journeys (for individuals, teams, or organizations) typically have a trigger point that inspires change. From here, it is critical to understand the causes and reasons that are blocking progress. Becoming aware of what is enabling you and hindering you, with any goal, enables you to best decide the changes that need to be made and where to start.

Looking at where you may need to start...

As you work towards planning how you can start engaging some of these behaviors at work, especially if you manage teams or have a role in leadership, here are some questions to think about. Your answers will help you get started in figuring out where you may want to begin!

Accountability

When things go wrong at work, do people throw each other under the bus?

Do employees at all levels take ownership over their actions, even when things go wrong?

What does the team language sound like when discussing failure?

Achievement

Do people have challenging yet achievable goals?

Do people feel as though they are continuously learning?

Do managers understand their employees' personal career goals?

Are people exposed to opportunities for growth--both personally and professionally?

Are meaningful achievements acknowledged in the right way for the employees?

Alignment of Task and Time

Do employees' work efforts align with their strengths as well as what they enjoy?

Are there opportunities to get involved in projects or activities that align with people's passion or what is meaningful to them?

Authenticity

Do people treat each other with respect?

Do people respond to challenging moments, even when emotions are high, with compassion?

Do people do what they say they will and see commitments through?

Do people represent their true, authentic self, by being open and honest?

Awareness

Do people tend to react quickly, or do they come across more thoughtful in their responses so that the outcome is the best possible--even in challenging situations?

Do people have inflated egos or an inflated sense of self-importance?

Are people aware of the feelings of others?

Basic Wellbeing and Self-Care

Even though there may be peak times and fires to put out, do people have generally sustainable workloads?

Are employees measured by the value they bring, the outcomes and objectives, rather than how long they are seen working, present or online?

Does leadership role model taking time for, and placing importance on, their health and self-care?

Is there access to healthful options, break spaces, and support for fitness activities?

Do people tend to make use of break spaces or take the time to have a break?

Mindful Practice

Do people tend to actively listen, or are they too busy thinking about their response, when in conversations?

Are people generally distracted and multi-tasking?

Are people in back-to-back meetings for most of the day?

Do people tend to eat at their desk during their workday?

Positive Outlook

Do people share stories about the successes of others, themselves, and the organization?

Are people aware of any social good the company is supporting or taking part in?

Do people seem energized around the office or is morale low?

Can you easily list five genuine positives about working for the organization?

Do managers promote positive energy? Or, do they seem to focus on the negative or amplify how negative situations are?

Purpose and Meaning

Do people understand the company's mission and brand values?

Do people understand how they play a role in the company's bigger picture?

Do people understand their customers, who they are, and how the company serves them?

During the hiring process, is alignment to cultural values taken into consideration?

What happens when someone, at any level, displays behaviors that are clearly against the company's cultural values? Are there any consequences?

Does leadership demonstrate the cultural values through their behaviors?

Relationships

Do people know each other as people, beyond just what they do for their job?

Are there opportunities for people to get to know each other and to get to know leadership?

How easy is it for people across the organization to work together?

Do people feel siloed in their functions, teams, or geographical location?

Solution Focus

What happens when a team, person, or the organization fails? Do they tend to ruminate and feel bad? Do other people pitch in to help solve the problem?

Do you have open conversations about lessons learned from projects, sales win-losses, and other moments that allow everyone to discuss what went right, what went wrong, and how you can do better next time?

Are people encouraged to bring forward their ideas and thoughts on improvements?

When there is a big failure, or challenging moment, how does leadership respond? How do they behave?

Do people have access to people that may be experiencing similar challenges?

Do people have access to people that are stronger in the areas that they wish to develop or are weaker in?

Are there opportunities for people to connect with mentors, advisors, and sponsors?

Do managers give clear, specific, actionable and frequent feedback?

Do managers solicit feedback and ensure employees feel their perspectives are welcomed and heard?

Look back at your answers and see where there are immediate opportunities for growth. Remember, oftentimes, our responses are based on how we see the world. This can cause a perception gap from what is happening in reality. When driving cultural change, it is important that the perspectives of leadership and employees at all levels are considered. It is also critical to identify the root causes as to why these behaviors are happening.

You will want to think about your organization's capacity for change, how ready and willing they are, if you need to quantify the business case to help you gain traction, and the effort it will take.

A final piece of advice, remember to take it step-by-step, try something, measure the results, get feedback, and see if it works.

ABOUT US

Sarah Deane

Sarah Deane is a writer, speaker, and innovator working at the intersection of Experience Design, Data Science, and Human Behavior. As a thought leader, she has traveled the globe leading workplace experience and employee engagement strategies for Fortune 500s and startups alike. Her methodologies and thoughts have been recognized across the industry, winning The Human Resources Today MVP Awards in the Leadership Development, Analytics, and "What's Next in HR" categories and being featured in IDC's PeerScape. She has been a featured speaker at SXSW, HRWest, Gartner's EITL Forum, America's Women Leadership Conference, Invent Your Future Conference, a guest lecturer at Stanford University Graduate School of Business, and can be seen on Huffington Post, Thrive Global, Business2Community, CIO Magazine, Training Industry, and other platforms on the topics of Leadership, A.I, Employee Experience, Customer Experience, and Wellbeing. Sarah holds a Master of Engineering in Computer Science and Artificial Intelligence and published her User Experience (UX) primer in 2014, providing rapid insight into understanding, developing, and applying strategic UX.

Sarah has travelled the globe studying human behavior as it pertains to experience, engagement, and productivity as well as spent hundreds of hours coaching leaders to unlock the power of their mind. As the creator and co-founder of MEvolution she is focused on helping people live life at full capacity.

James Mulkerin

James has spent over a decade in the domains of IT, support, and customer experience innovation, having experience that spans Fortune 500 to startups. He holds a Bachelor of Science degree in Management Information Systems. As the co-founder of MEvolution, he uses his vast and global knowledge of human interaction and IT services, to operationalize the model and tools created in secure, highly efficient, enterprise-grade solutions, that enables people and organizations to experience sustained change...really, really fast.

In creating this book, we also had some amazing editing contributions from Steven Tindle.

Steven Tindle

Steven is a Copy Editor, Marketing Strategist, and a true testament to the empowering impact of an energized mindset.

An aspiring writer, Steven started his journey with with us over 3 years ago when he came across the our tool. With a new-found energized mindset, he branched out in his career goals, personal goals, and all-around wellness.

Whether he's spending a night at the open mics or prepping his next piece of creative work, he puts his best attitude into everything he does.

A word on how we got here...

While I started out in A.I., with a talent for data and algorithms, after figuring out my love for human behavior and psychology, I moved into experience design. I met James while working on employee engagement and workplace experience at a Hewlett Packard--which spanned a vast global footprint and 320,000+ employees at the time. James had a background in operations, networking, DevOps, and customer experience.

We worked on several amazing workplace experience projects together from a technology, space, and human behavior perspective. Including, building the first Global IT 360 Experience Lab at Hewlett Packard's Headquarters, and traveling the globe to quantify and study employee experience. At one point, we were part of a team tasked with improving employee experience by a certain percentage and were handed a big report of 70 questions from a "Voice of the Workplace" survey that told us how satisfied and dissatisfied employees were with various statements. While shedding a light on possible areas to dig into, the results were not actionable and required further work and effort to understand what the issue really stemmed from.

I'll never forget the question, it was question 14 which stated, "I have the tools and processes needed to get my job done." We knew how many people agreed, disagreed, and how strongly--yet, we had to make people happier about this?! We saw a problem...the surveys were a nuisance for employees, they were not easily actionable for delivery teams, and as leaders, they were hard to make decisions from...not to mention the nuances of the question themselves. We thought, what if we could create a better way to measure, one that is more accurate and actionable? What if we could understand what needed to be stopped, started, and continued straight away to achieve the goal? What if the results actually revealed the roadmap?

After careers that spanned both the enterprise and start-up worlds, we founded our own company, EffectUX, based on helping people and organizations expedite the pace of change. We set to work developing a new methodology--one based on the creation of success models. A model for defining the best ecosystem in which a goal will naturally occur.

Think about losing weight. You measure where you are and your progress. Then, for optimal weight loss, you need: (1) the right environment e.g. access to healthy food, (2) the right mindset e.g. willpower to make the right decisions, and, (3) the right behaviors e.g. exercising for 20 minutes each day. Based on a lot of historic industry research and success/failure cases, we know what will work for the goal of losing weight. You will then tailor your plan, based on your unique circumstance--how much money you have, how much time you have, and how much effort you can put in. How much you have the optimal environment, mindset, and behaviors for you, will impact how quickly you see results and if those results are sustained. At EffectUX, we made achieving customer experience, employee experience, and leadership development work the same way--by providing the blueprint.

Hindsight is 20-20. We believe that foresight should be just as clear.

Our process utilizes techniques across several domains, such as-- experience design, algorithm engineering, data science, management of change, and human behavior. To create each model, we follow a process of (1) extensive research across structured and unstructured, primary and secondary data sources, (2) modeling, to identify the contributors to the goals, and (3) algorithm engineering to map indicators to insights. This technique enabled us to be successful at large-scale change and modernization by accurately diagnosing current state and driving rapid, continued results.

We spent many years creating measurement systems and consulting with Fortune 500's and start-ups to help them expedite the pace of change and make sense of their existing data across customer experience, employee experience, leadership and culture.

What happened next?

Through the research that led us to these 12 factors, we discovered where our passion, purpose, and talents intersected. While the journey into what makes people perform and feel their best was insightful, we found that we were intrigued by the power of human capacity. We discovered eight critical competencies that create capacity, as well as the blockers that work against them, leading us to shift our focus to helping people unlock, manage, and optimize their capacity for greater potential and possibilities.

Since then, much has happened. Especially, COVID. While the pandemic caused increased stress for many, it shone a spotlight on issues that existed long before. For us, this made our mission even more critical. To energize the world, one soul at a time. You can find us at: www.JoinThe MEvolution.com.

References & Further Reading

While hundreds of data sources were reviewed as a part of our research, here are some references that were cited within this book or which may provide additional reading.

Hartner, Lam; Mann, Annamarie. Gallup. The Right Culture: Not Just About Employee Satisfaction (2017, April 12) from https://www.gallup.com/workplace/236366/right-culture-not-employee-satisfaction.aspx

Anchor, Shawn; Green, Sarah. Harvard Business Review. Why a Happy Brain Performs Better (2010, November) from https://hbr.org/2010/11/why-a-happy-brain-performs-bet

Nolan, Liam. Medium. The Business Case for Happy Employees (2016, July 15) from https://medium.com/zealify-for-employers/the-business-case-for-happy-employees-4e334a65d13f

Morgan, Jacob. Harvard Business Review. Why the Millions We Spend on Employee Engagement Buy Us So Little (2017, March 10) from https://hbr.org/2017/03/why-the-millions-we-spend-on-employee-engagement-buy-us-so-little

Pelster, Bill; Johnson, Dani; Stempel, Jen; Vyer, Bernard van der. Deloitte. Careers and learning: Real time, all the time. 2017 Global Human Capital Trends (2017, February 28) from https://www2.deloitte.com/insights/us/en/focus/human-capital-trends/2017/learning-in-the-digital-age.html

Huhman, Heather. R. Entrepreneur. Half of All Companies Admit Their Employee Development Programs Are Outdated. Is Yours? (2018, May 10) from https://www.entrepreneur.com/article/312758